THE NEW AMERICAN LOGO

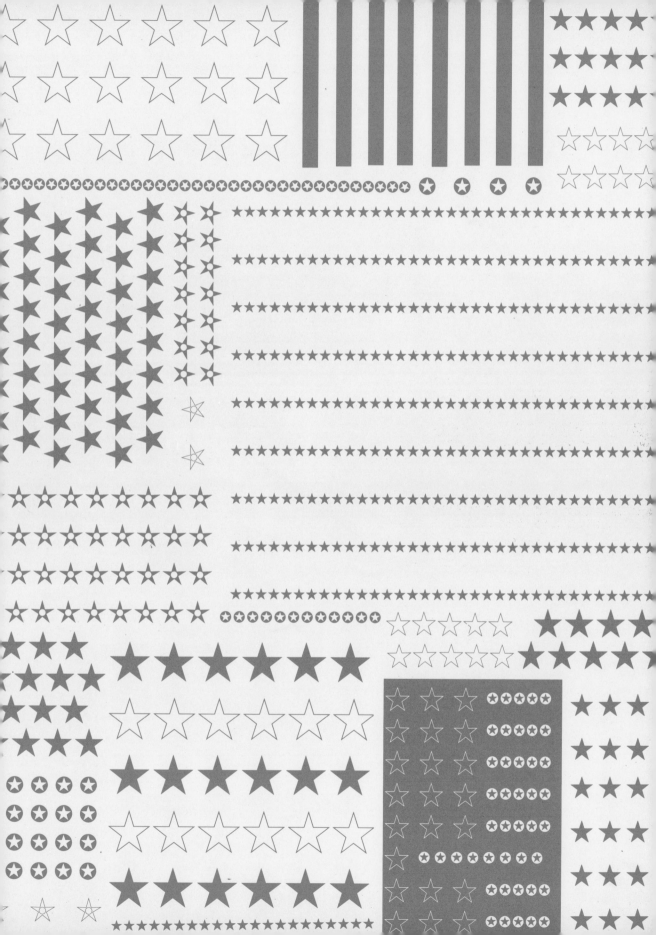

THE NEW AMERICAN LOGO

DESIGNED & EDITED
GERRY ROSENTSWIEG

INTRODUCTION BY
MARK FOX

PUBLISHED BY
MADISON SQUARE PRESS

C O N T E N T S

5

If, for a moment, you consider the American logo as a metaphor for sex, current logo design is moving beyond terse pecks on the cheek and finally getting somewhere interesting. It's about time.

Representational trademarks are a venerable tradition in the United States, but after World War II representation fell out of favor, first with painters, and then with designers. Einstein and technology were our keys to a happy, prosperous future—we won the war with the atomic bomb, remember—and the rationalist approach of Modernism was shaping everything from architecture to commercial art.

In logo design, the visual expression of the Modernist ideal was simple, geometric, and abstract. [Chermayeff and Geismar's 1960 octagon for Chase Manhattan Bank is one classic example.] Within this new climate, many companies found their images distinctly old fashioned, and they scrambled to jettison any vestiges of an embarrassing past: RCA's dog Nipper, Borden's cow Elsie, Mobil's Pegasus, NBC's peacock, and Reddy Kilowatt all got the ax.

Meanwhile, designers got fat from all the redesign work. From the 1950's through the 1970's they busily modernized, sanitized, reduced, abstracted, striped, and just plain ruined some of America's best trademarks. And of the thousands of new logos created during this period, a remarkable number are virtually indistinguishable due to their lack of visual referent and their reliance on geometric cliches.

For example, of the Modernist logos on the left, can you identify the symbol for the construction company, medical clinic, bank, office filing system, or insurance company?

Writing in *Design Issues*, Ann Tyler has observed that this type of simplified, geometric logo was developed to "represent the 'modern' corporation as a large, anonymous entity driven by technology and the values attributed to science." The flip side of this, of course, is that these marks also portray companies as emotionless and inhuman. [One notable exception: the CBS eye, designed by William Golden in 1958.]

§

In the late 1970's and early 1980's, after more than two decades of repressed logo design, something Gerry Rosentswieg refers to as "the New American Logo" spontaneously combusted itself into existence. Its emergence shouldn't have surprised anyone; pictorial symbolism was an obvious reaction to Modernist abstraction. But beyond this, there were some unique cultural events that led to change.

Gary Panter
The Screamers,
1977

Paul Rand aside, we can all thank the Sex Pistols and the revolution of punk for instigating changes in the music and fashion industries, and ultimately in the graphic design that serviced them. The urgency and sheer power of punk demanded a visual vocabulary that was different from disco, corporate musak, and polyester. This vocabulary manifested itself in the work of Pistols' designer Jamie Reid, the aesthetic of the office copier, and a revulsion to grids, Helvetica, and the Modernist vision. With Gary Panter's pivotal identity for the Screamers, logo design took a decidedly emotional turn. [Compare this to the logotype for the band Chicago, for instance.] And although the influence of Panter's logo wouldn't be immediately felt by multinational corporations seeking a new look, it would eventually percolate into the mainstream culture in the more commercially viable form of "New Wave" graphics.

Karl Schulpig
Moturba, 1927

Bob Aufuldish &
Eric Donelan
Big Cheese, 1993

In 1982 and 1985 Leslie Cabarga published his two-volume edition of *A Treasury of German Trademarks,* which introduced the logos of Karl Schulpig and Wilhelmwerk [c. 1920–1930] to America. Schulpig worked in a simple, geometric style, but, unlike the formalism of post-war American marks, his work is accessible and engaging. As his logo for Moturba demonstrates, Schulpig was unafraid of narrative, humor, and complex silhouettes.

Exposure to these early German trademarks has had a profound influence on a number of American designers, including Jay Vigon, Charles Spencer Anderson, and myself. [Paula Scher's remark from the jacket of volume two—"I have ripped off from this book more in the past year than any other"—is applicable to many of us.]

Then in 1984 Apple released the first Macintosh. Although the personal computer has been attacked for democratizing graphic design [if you own a mouse, you're a designer], it has led to some expressive and idiosyncratic work that wouldn't exist otherwise. One example: Big Cheese, illustrations in font format created by Bob Aufuldish and Eric Donelan. Although seemingly hand drawn, the Big Cheese logo is the result of a conscious subversion of the illustration software used to create it. This careful blend of technology and anarchy—which Aufuldish refers to as "a new humanism"—is particularly evident in the typography of magazines catering to sub and youth culture, foremost among them David Carson's *Ray Gun.*

§

Current logo design is thoroughly postmodern, which is another way of saying it bears the earmarks of retro. The best new logos are characterized by the same qualities as the old, pre-Modernist American trademarks of the 1920's–1940's. They are:

original

witty

accessible

mythic

idiosyncratic

emotive

memorable

The marks to the left are some of my favorites; they reflect this new—and old—approach to logo design. See if you have better luck discerning the identity for the donut shop, sweater manufacturer, media/entertainment company, restaurant, or surfwear company.

I am not suggesting that every abstract mark in America should be replaced by a globe, a little human, or even a happy face. Rather, I think that corporate executives [and the designers who service them] should relax, pump up the volume, and broaden their concept of what constitutes an appropriate image. Emotion is not a liability, and our humanity can be a cause for celebration rather than an admission of weakness. Posturing with an image of infallibility and omniscience in the 90's is silly; as Bob Dylan notes, "Even the President of the United States/Sometimes must have to stand naked."

Mark Fox
BlackDog
San Rafael, California

[Logo attributions can be found on page 212.]

1923
Sitos Hats
D: Wilhelm Deffke

1968
Planned Parenthood
World Population
D: Rudolph de Harak

1990
Restaurant Toulouse
D: Todd Waterbury
A: Duffy, Inc.

The logo, which has come full circle, has long been a choice assignment for graphic designers. First there were the quirky, personal marks that identified products and businesses in the first half of this century, then the corporate years brought abstract marks that were elegant, but signified little. And now, once again, the "new" logo is quirky and personal.

These logos, reflect the changes in American business as well. The identifying marks or logos of this century's early years were indicative of the individuality, quality and service those businesses provided. As business became more sophisticated, and more impersonal, so did the company logo.

Years of political and business scandals and corruption, plus a plethora of social and financial problems, have made simplistic identification desirable again. Large companies, as well as small, have adopted the "new" logo, often to combat the general bad reputation that business has acquired.

Many of the symbols in this collection are illustrations pressed into service as company identification. Even when a "new" logo is created by computer, it reflects the person who conceived it. These personal, human marks are memorable; they relate to people and make them comfortable. That is their function and that makes them important.

Gerry Rosentswieg, 1994

12

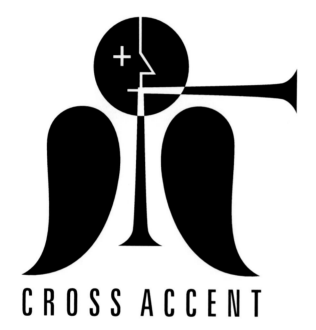

CROSS ACCENT

12.1

12.2

12.1
Robert Sirko
Indiana, 1992
R. Sirko Design
Symbol for a publication
for church musicians.

12.2
Thomas Vasquez
Texas, 1993
Brainstorm, Inc.
Symbol for a line of men's
grooming products.

13.1 - 13.3
Su Huntley/Donna Muir
California, 1990
Huntley/Muir Design
AD: MarySue Milliken/Susan Feiniger
Promotional symbols for a chain of
non-traditional Mexican restaurants.

13.4
Michael Vanderbyl
California, 1992
Vanderbyl Design
Symbol/illustration for a
fundraising project of the American
Center for Design.

13.5
Rick Tharp
California, 1992
Tharp Did It
Symbol for Fire & Ice, a peppermint
and red hot liqueur that implies one
should chase it with something cool.

13.6
Lanny Sommese/Kristin Breslin
Sommese
Pennsylvania, 1993
Sommese Design
Symbol for a jazz appreciation club.

13.1

13.4

13.2

13.5

13.3

13.6

14.1

14.2

14.1
Michael Vanderbyl
California, 1991
Vanderbyl Design
Symbol for a residential community
in Hawaii, The name Makani Kai
means ocean breeze.

14.2
Haley Johnson
Minnesota, 1991
Charles S. Anderson Design
AD: Charles S. Anderson
Symbol for Nike Mercury, a
running shoe.

14.3
Karl Hirschmann
Colorado, 1992
Reginald Wade Richey
Symbol for a marketplace near
Detroit. The symbol was inspired by
the old Lincoln/Mercury trademark.

15.1
Mark Fox
California, 1992
Black Dog
Mascot symbol, *Arrowhead*, for a TV
show, *"Name Your Adventure"*.

15.2
Haley Johnson
Minnesota, 1991
Charles S. Anderson Design
AD: Charles S. Anderson
The Nike Runner symbol used for
new product introduction.

15.3
Lisa Graff
New Mexico, 1992
Vaughn Wedeen Creative
AD: Steve Wedeen
Symbol for Network Commuter, a
telecommunications firm.

15.4
Steve Tolleson
California, 1989
Tolleson Design
Symbol for a computer company
annual report.

15.1

15.2

15

15.3

15.4

16.1

16.3

BARNEY TABACH

16.2

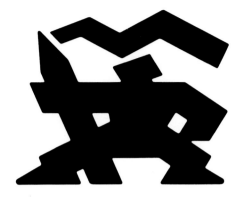

17.1

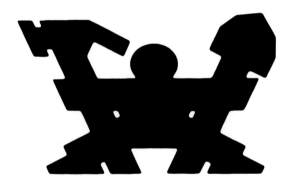

17.2

16.1
Tim Kovick
Tennessee.1992
Kovick, Logan, Fitzgerald
Symbol for a paint manufacturer.

16.2
John Sayles
Iowa, 1991
Sayles Graphic Design
A personal mark for an avid golfer.

16.3
Paul Woods
California, 1991
SBG Partners
Symbol for Loose Fit Jeans for
Levi Strauss & Co.

17.1
Charles S. Anderson/Haley Johnson
Minnesota, 1989
Charles S. Anderson Design
Symbol for Minneapolis College of
Art and Design. It depicts a figure
holding a pencil/flag waving an
abstract "M".

17.2
Kelly Ludwig
Missouri, 1992
Symbol for an excavation and
construction company.

17.3
Montine Selak
New York, 1991
Zebra Design
Symbol for a banking human
resources department. The symbol
implies that personnel will have to
stepout of their current rolls and take
on new responsibilities.

17.3

18.1

18.4

18.2

18.5

FX4U

18.3

18.6

18.1
Tracy Holdeman
Kansas, 1993
Love Packaging Group
AD: Brian Miller
Symbol for "*A Brush With Life*" a
fund raising art auction.

18.2
Charles S. Anderson/Todd Hauswirth
Minnesota, 1993
Charles S. Anderson Design
AD: Charles S. Anderson
Illus: Charles S. Anderson/Lynn Schulte
Symbol for concert producers who
raise funds for environmental action.

18.3
Hugh Whyte
New Jersey, 1992
Lehner & Whyte
AD: Donna Lehner
Illus: Hugh Whyte
Symbol for a fashion design company.

18.4
Tracy Holdeman
Kansas, 1992
Love Packaging Group
Symbol for a lawn care service.

18.5
Todd Fedell
Arizona, 1992
Todd Fedell Design
Symbol for Renegade Electronics.

18.6
Jay Vigon
California, 1993
AD: Paul Vega
Symbol for the *Envisions* conference.
It exhorts attendees to "Wallop
those wicked walls of mediocrity".

19.1
John Evans
Texas, 1991
Sibley/Peteet Design
Symbol for Jim's Gym.

19.2
James F. Kraus
Massachusetts, 1993
Art Guy Studios
AD: Maggie
Agcy: Larry Miller Productions
Symbol for a computer chip
manufacturers' new product.

19.3
David S. Rheinhardt
New Jersey, 1993
DSR Design
Symbol for a clothing line.

19.1

19.2

19.3

20.1

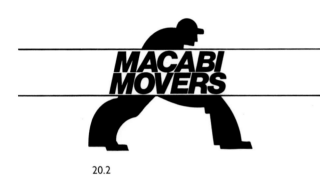

20.2

20.3

20.1
John O'Brien/Jay Vigon
California, 1993
Cimarron/Bacon/O'Brien
AD:Jeffrey Bacon/John O'Brien
Symbol which promises
powerful entertainment and
high technology.

20.2
Michael Stetson
New York, 1989
Symbol for a moving company.

20.3
Kevin Whaley
Minnesota, 1989
GrandPré and Whaley, LTD
Symbol for the creative department
of a printing firm.

21.1
Christine McFarren
California, 1990
Kowalski Designworks, Inc.
AD: Stephen Kowalski
Symbol for a bicycle messenger
service.

21.2
James F. Kraus
Massachusetts, 1992
Art Guy Studios
Symbol for a college radio station.
The illustration of the radio signal
beaming in a unique way. It signifies
on the edge music and a "kool dude".

21.3
Paul Munsterman
Texas, 1991
Swieter Design
AD: John Swieter
Symbol for leisurewear that
resembles surgical scrubs.

21.4 - 21.5
Rudiger Gotz
Minnesota, 1991
Duffy, Inc.
AD: Sharon Werner
Symbols for Hard Rock kids bicycles.

21.1

21.4

21.2

21.5

21.3

22.1

22.1
Art Chantry
Washington, 1984
Art Chantry Design
Symbol echoing German design for
this beer-drinking event.

23.1
Luis Fitch
Ohio, 1988
Luis Fitch Diseño
Symbol for a musical group.

23.2
Mary Scott
California, 1992
Maddocks & Company
AD: Frank Maddocks
Symbol for a vending machine
company.

23.3
Rick Yurk
California, 1992
James Robie Design Associates
AD: James Robie
Symbol for Native, a sportswear
company. The designer points out
that "we're all natives, it's just
that we forget- this logo is just
a reminder".

23.4 - 23 .5
Charles S. Anderson/Daniel Olson
Minnesota, 1990
Charles S. Anderson Design Co.
AD: Charles S. Anderson
Symbols for Earthwise, a line of
recycled paper products.

23.6
Cameron Woo
California, 1990
AT&T Design Group
AD: John Seminario
Special event identity for an
international marketing rally. "Willy
Loman meets Cassandre."

23.1

23.2

23.3

23.4

23.5

23.6

24.1
Stephen Guarnaccia/
Susan Hochbaum
New York, 1988
Studio Guarnaccia
Interchangeable symbols for a youth
oriented music company.

25.1
Kevin Akers
California, 1990
Burson-Marsteller
Symbol for a design newsletter.

25.2
Mary GrandPré/ Kevin Whaley
Minnesota, 1988
GrandPré & Whaley
Symbol for a veterinarian.

25.3
Mike Schmalz
Iowa, 1993
McCullough Graphics
Symbol for Newton, the race
mascot for a mountain bike downhill
race. These races are based on
gravity/speed. The symbol represents Newton discovering gravity.

25.4
Bennett Peji
California, 1990
Bennett Peji Design
Symbol for a catering and special
events company.

25.5
Kevin Akers
California, 1989
Burson-Marsteller
Symbol for Hilton Hotels
Bounceback Weekend package.

25.6
Kelly Allen
Texas, 1992
SullivanPerkins
AD: Ron Sullivan
Symbol for a children's mental
health organization.

24.1

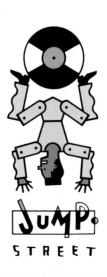

25.1

25.4

FEIST
ANIMAL
HOSPITAL

25.2

25.5

25.3

25.6

26.1

26.4

26.2

26.5

26.3

26.6

26.1
Joseph Glorioso, III
Maryland, 1993
Symbol for Pipeline Studios, "polished rawness and slightly off-kilter stability" are the elements.

26.2
Nicholas McAughey
Florida, 1993
Ringling Design Center
Symbol for a university book fair.

26.3
Mark Harakuji
California, 1990
Symbol for Alex Photography.

26.4
Debra Nichols
California, 1991
Debra Nichols Design
Symbol for a children's health club.

26.5
Todd Hart
Texas, 1993
Focus 2
Symbol for a fun, beach-culture radio station.

26.6
Todd Hart
Texas, 1993
Focus 2
Symbol for a hip photographer capable of handling big projects.

27.1 - 27.2
Dana Shields
California, 1992
CKS Partners
AD: Tom Suitor
Symbol for a multimedia software package. The "K-man" takes on various personalities when animated.

27.3
Kelly Allen
Texas, 1993
SullivanPerkins
AD: Ron Sullivan
Positive attitude symbol for a mental health organization.

27.4
Jeff Weithman
Oregon, 1993
Nike Design
Illus: Greg Maffei
This symbol is designed to reflect the energy, movement and total body conditioning of a new line.

27.1

27.2

27.3

27.4

28.1

28.2

28.3

28.1
Randy Burman
Florida, 1993
HE2.3
AD: Kurt Meredith
Agency: CreatAbility
Symbol for Child Care
Connection, a multi-ethnic family
support program.

28.2
Charles S. Anderson/
Todd Hauswirth
Minnesota, 1993
Charles S. Anderson Design Co.
Illus: Charles S. Anderson/
Lynn Schulte
Symbol for HOW Magazine's
international design competitition.

28.3
Lanny Sommese
Pennsylvania, 1991
Sommese Design
Symbol for Remodelers Workshop.

29.1 - 29.3
John Sayles
Iowa, 1989
Sayles Graphic Design
Icons for the studio illustrating its'
business philosophy.

29.4
Lanny Sommese
Pennsylvania, 1991
Sommese Design
AD: Lanny Sommese/ Kristin
Breslin Sommese
Symbol for Mr. Fix-it, a repairman
ready to run to the rescue.

29.5
Andrew Dolan
Washington, DC, 1993
Supon Design Group, Inc.
AD: Supon Phornirunlit
Symbol for National Community
AIDS Partnership.

29.6
Mark Sackett
California, 1993
Sackett Design
Illus: Clark Richardson
Symbol for Carelinc, a provider
of care consulting services to
corporations.

29.1

29.4

29.2

29.5

29.3

29.6

29

30.1

30.2

30.3

30.4

30.5

30.6

30

30.1
James Clifford Davis
California, 1992
Personal promotional symbol. The
mark shows "the designer with his
two most vital creative tools - his
brain and his computer. Hopefully in
that order."

30.2
Ken Loh
California, 1992
Evenson Design Group
AD: Stan Evenson
Proposed symbol for Private
Excercise.

30.3
Bill Gardner/Sonia Greteman
Kansas, 1991
Gardner + Greteman
Symbol for Poor Sports, a discount
sporting goods store.

30.4-30.5
Alan Lampe
Iowa, 1993
Younkers Advertising Department
Athletic department logos.

30.6
John Sayles
Iowa, 1992
Sayles Graphic Design
Symbol for a company that manages
worldwide information systems.

31.1
John Sayles
Iowa, 1992
Sayles Graphic Design
Symbol for a university event.

31.2
Kirk Richard Smith
Ohio, 1992
Firehouse 101 Design
Symbol for a clothing line.

31.1

31.2

32.1
Paula Wong
Washington, 1990
Aldus Creative Services
AD: Don Bergh
Symbol for delivering Beta
software quickly.

32.2
Christopher Klumb
New York, 1989
E. Christopher Klumb Associates, Inc.
Symbol for children's health care
services.

32.3
John Nishimoto
New York, 1992
John (NY)
"This mark signifies the ultimate sim-
plification to the essence of a design
problem/solution; or depersonalizing
the personal logo.

33.1
Gerry Rosentswieg
California, 1992
The Graphics Studio
Symbol for an adult gymnastics
program.

33.2
Bill Gardner/Sonia Greteman
Kansas, 1993
Gardner + Greteman
Symbol for a health food store.

33.3
Mark Fox
California, 1992
Black Dog
Promotional logo for jeans.

33.4
Kevin Whaley
Minnesota, 1992
GrandPré & Whaley
AD: Pat Wright
Agency: Business Incentives, Inc.
Logo for a company incentive
program.

33.5
Tracy Holdeman
Kansas, 1990
Gardner Greteman Mikulecky
AD: Sonia Greteman
Symbol for an artists representative.

33.6
Jon Flaming
Texas, 1992
Jon Flaming Design
Logo for a mens soccer team.

32.1

32.2

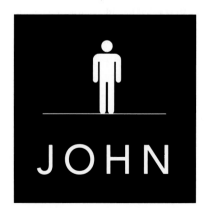

32.3

33.1

33.4

33.2

33.5

33.3

33.6

34.1

34.3

34.2

34.4

34.1
Cameron Woo
California, 1990
AT & T Graphics Group
Symbol for a newsletter column,
HealthNews.

34.2
Andrew Dolan
Washington DC, 1993
Supon Design Group
AD: Supon Phornirunlit
Symbol for the YMCA
membership campaign.

34.3
Randy Heil
Arizona, 1992
Randy Heil Design & Illustration
Symbol for The Image Guys, a com-
pany that produces camera ready art
for the advertising specialty business.

34.4
Ken Loh
California, 1992
Evenson Design Group
AD: Stan Evenson
Logo for a physical fitness club.

35.1
Bill Fricke
New Jersey, 1993
Graffic Jam
Personal symbol that implies "logos
aren't limited. It means to the viewer
- lighten up, leave the tags off"

35.2
Eric Rickabaugh
Ohio, 1990
Rickabaugh Graphics
Studio logo with a sense of humor.

35.1

35.2

36.1

36.3

36.2

36.4

36.5

36.1
Michael Brower
California, 1993
Brower Design
Symbol for Bod·e, a fitness
apparel company.

36.2
Jon Flaming
Texas, 1993
Jon Flaming Design
Symbol for a landscaping business.

36.3
Walter McCord
Kentucky, 1987
Choplogic
Symbol for a metaphysical
conference.

36.4
William Reuter/José Bila.
California, 1992
William Reuter Design
AD: William Reuter
Illus: José Bila
Symbol for an architects conference.

36.5
Mark Anderson
Missouri, 1990
Eilts Anderson Tracy
Symbol for a walk-a-thon sponsored
by a software developer.

37.1
Tim Robinson
Texas, 1991
Swieter Design
AD: John Swieter
Proposed symbol for leisurewear
that resembles medical scrubs.

37.2
Andrew Dolan
Washington DC, 1993
Supon Design Group
AD: Supon Phornirunlit
Symbol for the studio signifying
smart design.

37.3
Patrice Eilts
Missouri, 1991
Eilts Anderson Tracy
Symbol for the Union of Smaller
City Newspapers.

37.1

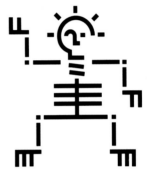

37.2

37.3

38.1

38.2

38.1
Jim Vogel/Paul Munsterman
Texas, 1991
Swieter Design
AD: John Swieter
Symbol for a sports therapy clinic.

38.2
Peter Horjus
California, 1993
Horjus Design
Symbol for Dutch Window
Washing Service.

39.1
Bennett Peji
California, 1992
Bennett Peji Design
Symbol for a women's
therapy group.

39.2
Steve Curry
California, 1992
Curry Design
Symbol for an aromatherapy and
skin care company.

39.3
Andrew Dolan
Washinton DC, 1993
Supon Design Group
AD: Supon Phornirunlit
Symbol for a health spa.

39.4
Rebecca Michaels
Pennsylvania, 1993
Design Partners
Symbol for Breastfeeding
Resources.

39.5
Rick Tharp
California. 1993
Tharp Did It
AD: Cerstin Cheatham
Illus: Susan Jaekel
Logo for an aromatherapy salon.

39.6
John Patterson
Kansas, 1991
BTDesign
AD: Carey Treanor
Symbol for a center for obstetrics
and gynecology.

39.1

Breastfeeding
R E S O U R C E S

39.4

39.2

39.5

39.3

39.6

40.1

40.2

40.3

40.1
Kristin Breslin Sommese
Pennsylvania, 1991
Sommese Design
Symbol for women's awareness
week at a college. The woman's hair
relates to the earth, the breast to
the sun and the wide hips to the
concept of "Mother Earth".

40.2
Christine Nasser
California, 1990
Christine Nasser Design
Artists personal symbol.

40.3
John Sayles
Iowa, 1993
Sayles Graphic Design
Logo for a packaging manufacturer,
specifically for cosmetics.

41.1 - 41.3
Richard Lee Heffner
Washington DC, 1993
Supon Design Studio
AD: Supon Phornirunlit
Symbols used in ads for the studio.

AS WITH MAGIC, THERE'S A SECRET TO GOOD DESIGN.

41.1

41.2

41.3

42.1

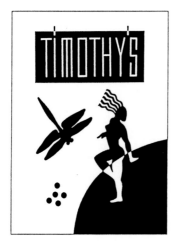

42.2

42.4

42.5

42.3

42.1 - 42.2
Walter McCord
Kentucky, 1986
Choplogic
Symbols for a restaurant.

42.3
Sue Harvey
Pennsylvania, 1990
Lynell Wilcha Design
Logo for a music publishing company
that specializes in calypso music.

42.4
Donna Lehner/Hugh Whyte
New Jersey, 1993
Lehner & Whyte
Logo for environmental
T-shirt design.

42.5
Randy Robinson
Missouri, 1993
Kuhn & Wittenborn Advertising
A summer program which encour-
ages students to think in new ways.
The figure growing and changing
represents the empowerment of
learning.

43.1
Jeffrey L. Dever
Maryland, 1993
Dever Designs Inc.
Mark which symbolizes women of
differing ages and races united in
ministry.

43.2
Elizabeth Rodriguez
New York, 1993
Another Vampire Production
Logo for design firm that handles
print, film and video.

General
Conference
Women's
Ministries

43.1

ANOTHER VAMPIRE PRODUCTION

43.2

44.1

44.2

44.3

44.4

44.1-44.3
Eric Rickabaugh
Ohio, 1989
Rickabaugh Graphics
Logo for an opera company's season.

44.4
John Sayles
Iowa, 1992
Sayles Graphic Design
Logo for a western mobile deli.

45.1
Bill Gardner/Sonia Greteman
Kansas, 1991
Gardner + Greteman
Logo for a printing company.

45.2
Scott Mires
California, 1993
Mires Design, Inc.
Illus: Tracy Sabin
Logo for illuminated footwear.

45.3
Teri Klass/Wendy Church
California, 1991
Vandenburg & Company
Logo for fast food restaurant,
Muscle Beach Burgers.

45.1

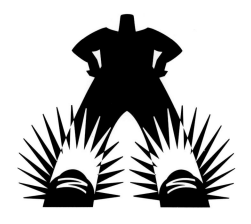

45.2

45.3

46.1

46.2

EXCALIBUR

46.3

46.1
Tracy Holdeman
Kansas, 1992
Love Packaging Group
Logo for a supplier and printer of
corrugated packaging.

46.2
Ed Anderson
Ohio, 1992
Communica
Logo for a company that
relines barrels.

46.3
Michael Johnson
Minnesota, 1993
Designkor
Illus: Mark Herman
Logo for a barbershop quartet.

47.1
Robert Brook Allen
New York, 1991
Gregg & Associates
Logo for a children's fitness
program at a preschool.

47.2
David Kampa
Texas, 1993
Kampa Design
AD: Turk Pipkin
Mark for "Softshoe" a writing,
publishing and juggling company,
indicating "the old song and dance".

47.3
Glenn Parson
California, 1992
Icon West
Logo for a computer service bureau.

47.4
Frank X. Doyle
California, 1992
Silicon Graphics Creative
"Artisan Man" the mark represents
visualization of history-thought,
vision, desire, tools and electronic
media.

raymore fun and fitness program

47.1

47.3

47.2

47.4

V I S U A L   A S Y L U M

48.1

S E A F A I R 1 9 9 3

48.2

48.1
Amy Levine
California, 1993
Visual Asylum, a graphic design firm.
AD: MaeLin & Amy Levine

48.2
Jeff Welsh/Traci Daberko/
Jon Cannell/Barb Ferguson
Washington, 1993
The Leonhardt Group
AD: Janet Krise
Symbol for a family oriented multi-
cultural festival.

49.1
Bruce Edwards
Minnesota, 1993
Rapp Collins Communications
Symbol for "The Tribe" a
musical group.

49.2
Sharon Werner
Minnesota, 1989
Duffy, Inc.
Illus: Sharon Werner/Lynn Schulte
Symbol for a French restaurant with
an art deco theme.

49.3
John Sayles
Iowa, 1991
Sayles Graphic Design
Logo for an art therapist.

49.4
James F. Kraus
Massachusetts, 1992
Art Guy Studios
AD: Scott Love
Recycling symbol for an earth
conscious skin care products
manufacturer.

49.5
James F. Kraus
Massachusetts, 1992
Art Guy Studios
AD: Scott Love
Symbol for Botanical Rex
Skin Care Products.

49.6
Deborah Martin
New York, 1993
Martin Design
Symbol for a company that raises
funds through entertainment venues.

49.1

49.4

49.2

49.5

ART THERAPIST

49.3

TWO BLACK GIRLS

49.6

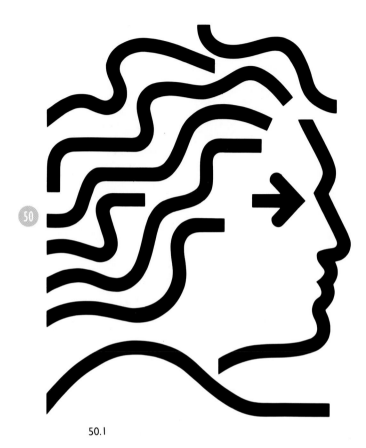

50.1

50.2

50.1
Eric Rickabaugh
Ohio, 1990
Rickabaugh Graphics
Symbol for "Directions for Youth"
an organization that helps direct
troubled teens.

50.2
Bill Basler/Colleen Wendling
Iowa, 1993
Basler Design Group
Symbol for "Offshore Concepts",
a nautical mercury, the symbol for
custom race boats.

51.1
John Evans
Texas, 1989
Sibley/Peteet Design
Symbol for "Simply for Sports"
a sportswear department of
J.C. Penney.

51.2
Peter Horjus
California,
Horjus Design/Illustration
Designers personal mark.

51.3
John Swieter/Paul Munsterman
Texas, 1993
Swieter Design
Logo for Consolidated Courier
Company.

51.4
John Sayles
Iowa, 1988
Sayles Graphic Design
Symbol for a unisex hair salon.

51.1

51.2

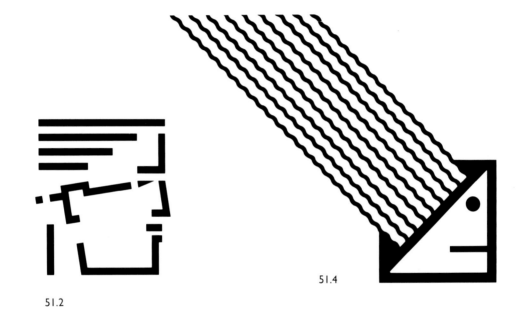

51.4

51.3

Bewear

52.1

52.4

52.2

52.5

52.3

52.6

52.1
Mark Fox
California, 1993
Black Dog
Logo for a clothing company.

52.2
Todd Hauswirth
Minnesota, 1991
Charles S. Anderson Design
Personal logo for a graphic designer
that specializes in computers.

52.3
Mark Fox
California, 1993
Black Dog
AD: Robin Lynch/Elektra Records
Symbol for a CD, "The Sound of
White Noise".

52.4
Irene Yap
California, 1992
Evenson Design Group
Logo for a non-profit organization
that teaches people how to read.

52.5
James F. Kraus
Massachusetts, 1992
Art Guy Studios
Designer/Illustrator's personal mark.

52.6
Mark Fox
California, 1992
Black Dog
A symbol for anti-piracy campaign.

53.1
Peter Horjus
California, 1991
Horjus Design
Symbol for a college club involved
in fine art, music, literature and
dramatic arts - a symbol that
screams for attention

53.2
Scott Ray
Texas, 1992
Peterson & Company Symbol for
Dallas Repertory Theatre.

53.3
Mark Fox
California, 1991
Black Dog
Symbol for a linotronic output
service bureau, his motto: I am
highly resolved.

53.1

53.2

53.3

54.1

54.4

54.2

54.5

54.3

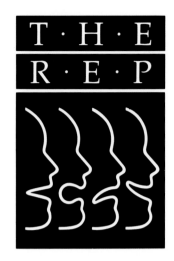

54.6

54.1
John Evans
Texas, 1993
John Evans Design
Symbol for Jeanne Evans/actress.

54.2
James L. Selak
New York, 1992
Zebra Design
Symbol for customer communications for an international company that manufacturers documenting equipment.

54.3
Scott Johnson
Indiana, 1990
Dean Johnson Design
Symbol for a doctor.

54.4
Dan Weeks
Ohio, 1992
Weeks & Associates
Symbol for a small community theatre.

54.5
Glenn Sakamoto
California, 1992
Evenson Design Group
AD: Stan Evenson
Symbol for a three prinicipal accounting firm.

54.6
Don Kline/Dennis Favello
New York, 1991
Don Kline Co.
Symbol for a global telecommunications company, Teleglobe.

55.1
Bob Donovan
Colorado, 1993
Bob Coonts Design Group
AD: Bob Coonts
Symbol for Voice It Technologies.

55.2
Neil Powell
Minnesota, 1992
Duffy, Inc.
Logo for ergonomically designed office products.

55.3
Mark Fox
California, 1993
Black Dog
Symbol for an artists representative.

55.1

55.2

55.3

56.1
Kristin Breslin Sommese
Pennsylvania, 1993
Sommese Design
Symbol for womens awareness week
at Penn State.

56.2
John Swieter/Jim Vogel
Texas, 1991
Swieter Design
Symbol/logo for a design firm.

56.3
Tracy Holdeman/Brian Miller
Kansas, 1993
Love Packaging Group
Symbol for Founders Day celebra-
tion at Wichita College.

57.1
Becca Bootes
California, 1992
Hershey Associates
Symbol for a sponsor of gay
pride events.

57.2
Mark Wood
California, 1993
Mark Wood Design Office
Symbol representing an "ice" man
and the three point positioning of ice
hockey forwards.

57.3
Richard Lee Heffner
Washington, D.C., 1992
Supon Design Group, Inc.
AD: Supon Phornirunlit
Symbol/logo for a gift shop.

57.4
Brian Collins
Minnesota, 1993
Gardner Design
AD: Nancy Gardner
Illus: Yas Bakshian
Symbol for a design firm. Figure with
tools is referred to as the "design
guy", and implies that design is a peo-
ple function.

57.5
Kevin Akers
California, 1988
Agency: Burson Marsteller
Symbol for Aria Software.

57.6
Ron Kellum
New York, 1992
Ron Kellum Inc.
Logo for Topix, a computer
animation company.

56.1

56.2

56.3

57.1

57.4

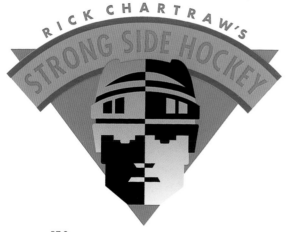

57.2

57.5

57.3

57.6

58.1

58.4

58.2

58.5

58.3

58.6

58.1
John Evans
Texas, 1988
Sibley/Peteet Design
Symbol for a game, the confetti com-
ing out of the head symbolizes the
"party in your brain" theme.

58.2
Bill Gardner/Sonia Greteman
Kansas, 1993
Gardner + Greteman
Symbol for "Jakes Attic", a childrens
science TV show.

58.3
Richard Boynton
Virginia, 1993
Boynton Design
Symbol for Prephead, a free-lance,
pre-press production designer.

58.4
Stan Evenson
California, 1992
Illus: Glenn Sakamoto
Evenson Design Group
Proposed symbol for Learning
Concepts Group.

58.5
John Evans
Texas, 1990
Sibley/Peteet Design
Symbol representing the excitement
of a video game player, for a game
manufacturer.

58.6
John Evans
Texas, 1993
Sibley/Peteet Design
Masthead symbol for a financial
newsletter, *Dollars & Sense*.

59.1
Richard Boynton
Virginia, 1993
Boynton Design
Symbol for environmentality.

59.2
Joe Rattan/Greg Morgan
Texas, 1993
Joseph Rattan Design
Symbol for Cyber Productions, a
multi-media production service. It is
meant to describe an industry that
utilizes all of ones senses.

59.3
Mark Fox
California, 1993
Black Dog
AD: Janet Covey
Symbol for a mangement
consulting firm.

59.1

59

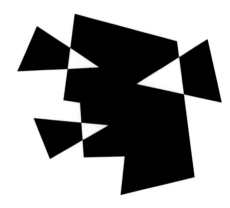

59.2

59.3

60.1

60.2

60.3

60.1
Mark Fox
California, 1992
Black Dog
AD: Sharon Anderson
"Tip" Icon for software manual.

60.2
James F. Kraus
Massachusetts, 1992
Art Guy Studios
Symbol for design studio, stating
clearly that art is protected,
copyrighted.

60.3
Mark Fox
California, 1992
Black Dog
Symbol for a production of "Jesus
Christ Superstar".

61.1-61.8
Gerry Rosentswieg
California, 1993
The Graphics Studio
AD: Jan Roberts
Proposed icon for shopping bags,
barricades and holiday decor at a
major mall.

61.9
Gerry Rosentswieg
California, 1993
The Graphics Studio
AD: Sandra L. Joseph
Personal icon for a talent manage-
ment firm.

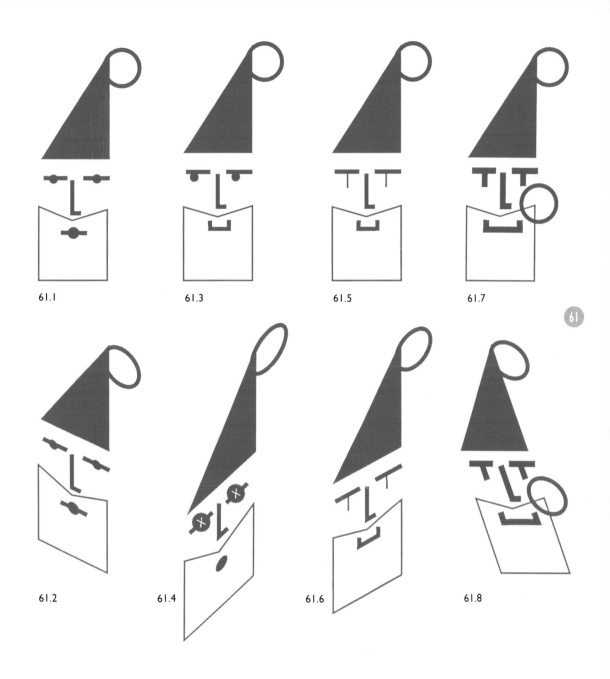

61.1

61.3

61.5

61.7

61.2

61.4

61.6

61.8

61.9

62.1

62.3

62.2

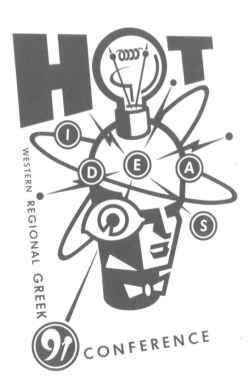

62.4

63.1

63.2

63.3

62.1
Todd Waterbury
Minnesota, 1992
Duffy, Inc.
Illus: Todd Waterbury/Lynn Schulte
Symbol/logo for a liquor.

62.2
Rudiger Gotz
Minnesota, 1991
Duffy, Inc.
AD: Joe Duffy
Illus: Rudiger Gotz/Lynn Schulte
Brand identity for a men's clothier.

62.3
Greg Rattenborg
Colorado, 1993
Bob Coonts Design Group
AD: Bob Coonts
Symbol for a doctor specializing in
facial reconstructive surgery.

62.4
John Sayles
Iowa, 1990
Sayles Graphic Design
Symbol for an idea exchange
conference, Hot Ideas.

63.1
Tracy Holdeman
Kansas, 1992
Love Packaging Group
Symbol for the graphic design
department. of a packaging
manufacturer.

63.2
Tracy Holdeman
Kansas, 1992
Love Packaging Group
Symbol for sales/service department
of Love Box Company.

63.3
Jon Flaming
Texas, 1993
Jon Flaming Design
Symbol for a bicycle repair and ser-
vice company, Ken's Bicycle Service.

64.1

64.2

64.1
Jon Flaming
Texas, 1992
Jon Flaming Design
Symbol for Theatre 3.

64.2
John Smeaton
California, 1992
The Mednick Group
AD: Scott Mednick
Logo/symbol for a tie manufacturer.

65.1 - 65.2
Jon Flaming
Texas, 1993
Jon Flaming Design
Icons for Neiman-Marcus
departments.

65.3
Jeanne Greco
New York, 1989
Caffe Greco Design
Symbol for The Fragrance Shoppe, a
manufacturer of bath and beauty
products.

65.1

65.2

65.3

66.1

66.4

66.2

66.5

66.3

66.6

66

66.1
John Sayles
Iowa, 1993
Sayles Graphic Design
Symbol for a software company that
deals with customer satisfaction surveys.

66.2
Colm Sweetman
California, 1992
Silicon Graphics Creative
AD: Frank X. Doyle
Symbol showing user fascination with
the images on the computer monitor-
the theme for a conference.

66.3
John Sayles
Iowa, 1992
Sayles Graphic Design
Symbol/logo for a mexican
restaurant/nightclub.

66.4
John Sayles
Iowa, 1992
Sayles Graphic Design
Symbol/logo for a medical
research organization.

66.5
John Sayles
Iowa, 1993
Sayles Graphic Design
Symbol/logo for Annie Meacham
Creative, a freelance writer.

66.6
Mark Fox
California, 1988
Black Dog
Proposed logo for a donut chain.

67.1
James L. Selak
New York, 1991
Zebra Design
Symbol for a commercial real estate
firm. "With the nose and head to
find the right property".

67.2
Mark Fox
California, 1991
Black Dog
Logo for a mexican restaurant,
Carlita's portrait is constructed with
two exclamation points - one invert-
ed in keeping with spanish usage.

67.3
Mary Lou Morreal
California, 1992
Morreal Graphic Design
Symbol/logo for a distinctive
hair salon.

HortonCavey

67.1

67.2

Hey Saylor

67.3

68.1

68.4

68.2

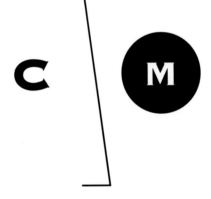

68.5

68.3

68.6

69.1

69.2

69.3

68.1
John Heiden
California, 1987
John Heiden Design
Logo for promotional CD.

68.2
Doug Zimmerman/Rick John
Iowa, 1993
Doug Zimmerman Illustration
Personal logo for an illustrator.

68.3
Todd Waterbury
Minnesota, 1990
Duffy, Inc.
AD: Joe Duffy
Logo for a french fast
food restaurant.

68.4
Sharon K. Hanley
Washington, 1987
S.K. Hanley Design
Logo for a tee shirt/silk screen
printing company - Lutz.

68.5
Dana Shields
California, 1993
CKS Partners
AD: Andy Dreyfus
Logo for an opthalmologist,
Dr. Charles Merker,

68.6
Gerry Rosentswieg
California, 1992
The Graphics Studio
Proposed logo for Children's
Hospital, Los Angeles.

69.1-69.3
Mark Fox
California, 1991
Black Dog
Illus: 69.1 Gary Baseman, 69.2 Greg
Clarke, 69.3 Mark Fox
Manly logos for Richard Manley, a
writer. Gary Baseman created the
angst-ridden man for the letterhead,
Greg Clarke illustrated the man lost in
thought for the envelope, and Mark
Fox created the monocled man for the
business card/bookmark. Look closely;
Freudian symbols abound.

70.1

70.4

70.7

70.2

70.5

70.8

70.3

70.6

70.9

70

70.1-70.9
Su Huntley/Donna Muir
California, 1990
Huntley & Muir
Icons for the Border Grill acknowl-
edging the food and spirit of the real
Mexico-staying carefully away from
"Tex-Mex Corn".

71.1
Luis Fitch
Ohio, 1989
Luis Fitch Diseño
Symbol for an optical clinic.

71.2
Ken Loh
California, 1992
Evenson Design Group
AD: Stan Evenson
Proposed symbol for Learning
Concepts Group-characterizing
enlightenment, interaction and vision.

71.3
Todd Hart
Texas, 1993
Focus 2
AD: Todd Hart/Shawn Freeman
Symbol/logo for a two person
graphic design studio.

71.1

71.2

71.3

72.1

72.2

72.3

72.4

S C H W A R T Z

P H O T O G R A P H Y

72.5

72.6

72.7

73.1

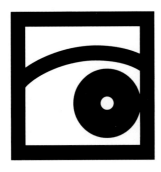

73.2

POINTE

OF

VIEW

73.3

72.1
Kevin Whaley
Minnesota, 1993
GrandPré & Whaley Ltd.
Symbol for Litho Prep, Inc.

72.2
Dan Flynn
New Mexico, 1993
Vaughn Wedeen Creative
AD: Dan Flynn/Steve Wedeen
Symbol for a photo filing system.

72.3
Mark Krumel
Ohio, 1992
Rickabaugh Graphics
Symbol for photographer, Greg Sailor.

72.4
David Zauhar
Minnesota, 1993
Zauhar Design
Ill: David Zauhar/Jack Wilcox
Symbol/logo for Scott Gatzke Photography.
Initials make up the lens aperture/eye.

72.5
Aaron Segall
Missouri, 1993
Symbol/logo for a photographer.

72.6
Kevin Whaley
Minnesota, 1991
GrandPré & Whaley Ltd.
Symbol for an electric security sensor
used for the protection of paintings.

72.7
Margo Chase
California, 1992
Margo Chase Design
AD: Jill Taffet
Logo for E! Entertainment Television.

73.1
Lee Perrault
New Hampshire, 1992
Via Design Inc.
Logo for a sleep evaluation facility.

73.2
Toni Schowalter
New Jersey, 1990
Schowalter Design
Symbol for Decision Strategies
International, management consultants.

73.3
Don Weller
Utah, 1992
The Weller Institute for the Cure
of Design, Inc.
Logo for a real estate development.

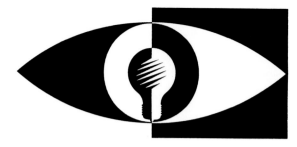

74.1

74.2

74.3

74.4

74.1
Ken Shafer
Washington, 1992
Ken Shafer Design
Symbol for an art school.

74.2
Gerald Reis
California, 1991
Gerald Reis & Company
Logo for column in a museum
newsletter.

74.3
Lynda Drebi, Carey Jones,
Ryoichi Yotsumoto
California, 1993
Laura Coe Design Associates
AD: Laura Coe Wright
Illus: Ryoichi Yotsumoto
Masthead for the Communicating
Arts Group newsletter.

74.4
Rick Yurk
California, 1992
James Robie Design Associates
AD: James Robie
Logo/symbol for a publisher of retail
stationery items.

75.1
Dan McNulty
California, 1993
McNulty & Company
Logo for a line of optical lenses.

75.2
Steve Curry
California, 1992
Curry Design
Logo for Imagine Films.

75.3
Richard Cassis
Illinois, 1993
SPARC
Logo/identity for a software product.

75.4
Bill Gardner/Sonia Greteman/
Karen Hogan
Kansas, 1993
Gardener + Greteman
Symbol for Guillaume Garrigue,
photographer.

75.5
Richard Wilks
California, 1992
Studio Wilks
Logo for a photojournalist,
Scott Varley.

75.6
James F. Kraus
Massachusetts, 1992
Art Guy Studios
"An eye on the world" for a
community recycling logo.

75.1

75.4

75.2

75.5

75.3

75.6

75

76.1

76.4

76.2

76.5

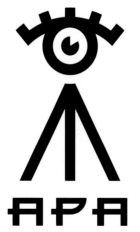

APA

76.3

76.6

76.7

76.1
Patricia McShane
California, 1993
M.A.D.
Symbol for a conference on
computer freedom and privacy.

76.2
Kent Dicken
Indiana, 1993
Dicken or Dicken
Proposed logo for permanant
cosmetics.

76.3
Mark Fox
California, 1992
Black Dog
Symbol/logo for Advertising
Photographers of America.

76.4
Mary Lou Morreal
California, 1990
Morreal Graphic Design
Symbol for a photography awards
exhibition.

76.5
David Zanhar
Minnesota, 1991
Zanhar Design
Symbol for RPM Video Production.

76.6
Kevin Akers
California, 1992
Design with Personality
Personal logo for a video producer,
Bill Emberly.

76.7
Peter Horjus
California, 1993
Horjus Design
Symbol for an optometrist

77.1
Debra Nichols/Kelan Smith
California, 1991
Debra Nichols Design
Illus: Mark Schroeder
Personal mark for a real estate
developer.

77.2
Todd Childers
North Carolina, 1992
Todd Childers Graphic Design
Logo/symbol for an upscale
eyeglass store.

77.3
Dana Shields
California, 1992
CKS Partners
AD: Tom Suiter
Symbol for a publisher.

RICHARD MENDELSOHN

77.1

77.2

CHRONICLE BOOKS

77.3

78.1
Don Weller
Utah, 1992
The Weller Institute for the Cure
of Design
Symbol for a masseur indicating the
magic fingers of massage.

78.2
Mark Fox
California, 1992
Black Dog
AD: Roz Romney
An industrial strength mark for
The Gap Jeans label.

79.1
Kevin Whaley
Minnesota, 1993
GrandPré & Whaley, Ltd.
AD: Kevin Whaley/Mary GrandPré
Symbol for a design studio.

79.2
Bill Gardner/Sonia Greteman
Kansas, 1992
Gardner + Greteman
Symbol for Wichita Industries and
Services for the Blind.

79.3
Lanny Sommese/Kristin Breslin
Sommese
Pennsylvania, 1990
Sommese Design
Symbol for an organization of artists.

79.4
Stewart Monderer/Kathleen Smith
Massachusetts, 1993
Stewart Monderer Design, Inc.
Symbol for Generations, a voice mail
software product.

79.5
Mark Fox
California, 1992
Black Dog
Proposed mark for the rock opera,
Jesus Christ, Superstar.

79.6
Kevin Whaley
Minnesota, 1989
GrandPré & Whaley, Ltd.
Symbol for a volunteer booster
organization.

78.1

78.2

79.1

79.4

79.2

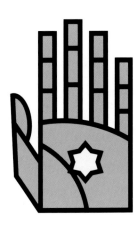

79.5

79.3

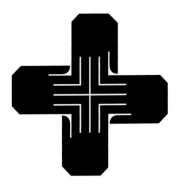

79.6

80.1

80.2

80.3

80.1
John Swieter/Kevin Flatt
Texas, 1992
Swieter Design
Personal mark for a graphic
design firm.

80.2
José Bila Rodriguez/Bill Reuter
California, 1992
William Reuter Design
Symbol for a management consultant
group, showing the importance of
human touch on the coporate world.

80.3
Ken Loh
California, 1993
Evenson Design Group
AD: Stan Evenson
Symbol for "American Gladiators"
an athletic television show.

81.1
Mark Fox
California, 1991
Black Dog
AD: Judi Radice
Symbol for use on T-shirts for Earth
Day, 1991. This mark depicts the
earth as an integral part of the
human hand. I was trying to illustrate
the thought that there is no separa-
tion between us and the planet; what
we do to it, we do to ourselves. It
was accompanied by the text "Treat
the Earth Well".

81.2
Christine Haberstock
California, 1993
Christine Haberstok Illustration
Symbol for photographer,
Hervé Pasquet.

81.3
Michael Osborne
California, 1991
Michael Osborne Design
Symbol for American Craft Council.

81.4
Jean Mogannam/Rick Tharp
California, 1992
Tharp Did It
Symbol for an interior design firm
"To Design".

81.5
Robin Cox
California, 1992
Cindy Slayton Creative
Symbol/logo for an animation
company.

81.1

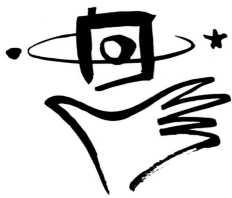

81.2

81.3

DESIGN

81.4

BIG
HAND

81.5

82.1

82.2

82.3

82.1
Dino Bernardi
California, 1992
Atelier 85
Symbol for a theatre production about Los Angeles - a city divided by culture and violence - is united in common dreams, hopes and faith in the future.

82.2
Mark Fox
California, 1991
Black Dog
AD: Richard Woo
Symbol for "Project Change", a funding initiative of The Levi Strauss Foundation, created to reduce racism. The symbol depicts the transformation of an arrow into an olive branch.

82.3
Linda Warren
California, 1992
Warren Design Group
Symbol for the UCLA alumni publication, depicting the accomplishments of graduates for forty years.

83.1
Linda Prosche
Illinois, 1993
Prosche Design
Symbol for a podiatrist.

83.2
Michael Carr
Illinois, 1990
Michael Carr Design
Symbol for a podiatry group.

83.3
Joe Parsley
Oregon, 1992
Nike Design
Illus: Joe Parsley/Davd Gill/ John Norman
Symbol for the recycling of shoe outsoles.

83.4
David Zauhar
Minnesota, 1993
Zauhar Design
Ill: David Zauhar/Jack Wilcox
Symbol for a chiropractic clinic.

83.5
Karen Dendy
Massachusetts, 1992
Barrett Design Incorporated
Symbol for EXOS, Inc. a health care instrumentation company.

83.1

83.4

83.2

83.5

83.3

84

84.1

84.2

84.4

84.3

84.5

85.1

85.2

85.3

84.1
Steven Guarnaccia
New York, 1991
Steven Guarnaccia
Symbol for a company that creates
music for advertising.

84.2
Tracy Holdeman/Sherri Laughlin
Kansas, 1993
Laughlin and Holdeman
Symbol for a garage that specializes
in motorcycle repair and restoration.

84.3
Keith Pucinelli/Heidi Palladino
New York, 1993
Pucinelli Design
Pictogram personal mark
for a graphic design firm.

84.4
Donna Lehner/Hugh Whyte
New Jersey, 1993
Lehner & Whyte
Symbol for a T-shirt design company.

84.5
Richard Rose
South Carolina, 1993
Rose Design
Symbol/logo for an organization of
owners/breeders of English Bull
Terrier dogs.

85.1
Michael Schwab
California, 1991
Michael Schwab Design
Symbol for new RCA equipment.

85.2
Robert Sirko
Indiana, 1991
R. Sirko Design
Symbol/logo for a manufacturer of
pet safety supplies.

85.3
Mark Fox
California, 1992
Black Dog
Personal symbol "Dogboy" he's
located somewhere between Lassie
and Einstein in Darwin's evolutionary
scheme-not unlike the designer.

86.1

86.2

DOGSTAR

86.3

86.4

Madeleine Clark

representative

86.5

86.6

86.1
Mark Fox
California, 1993
Black Dog
AD: Paul Curtin
Agency:Goodby, Berlin & Silverstein
Symbol/mascot for a cable TV
channel. His name is X-static.

86.2
Mark Fox
California, 1993
Black Dog
AD: Paul Curtin
Agency:Goodby, Berlin & Silverstein
Symbol/mascot for a cable TV
channel. His name is Re-run,

86.3
Rodney Davidson
Alabama, 1993
Dogstar Design & Illustration
Symbol for a design studio.

86.4
Michael Schwab
California, 1992
Michael Schwab Design
AD: Amanda Marcus
Symbol for a school whose team
is the Mustangs.

86.5
Margo Chase
California, 1993
Margo Chase Design
Symbol for an artist rep who "jumps
through hoops" for her clients.

86.6
Bill Gardner/Sonia Greteman
Kansas, 1993
Gardner + Greteman
Symbol for Colorations, a
service bureau.

87.1
Don Weller
Utah, 1993
Weller Institute for the Cure of
Design, Inc.
Symbol for Western Exposure,
a riding attire shop.

87.2
Linda Lawler
California, 1992
Linda Lawler Design
Symbol for an invitation to
a seminar on printing.

87.3
Mark Fox
California, 1992
Black Dog
Symbol for a color output
service, "a horse of a different
color" campaign.

87.1

87.2

87.3

88.1

88.4

88.2

88.5

88.3

88.6

88

88.1
David Kampa
Texas, 1990
Kampa Design
Symbol for Wildcat Records.

88.2
Mark Fox
California, 1993
Black Dog
Symbol for Xcat, a clothing line.

88.3
Saul Bass/Michael Cervantes
California, 1991
Bass/Yager
Symbol for a flashlight line.

88.4
Bill Gardner/Sonia Greteman
Kansas, 1990
Gardner + Greteman
Symbol for a dentist.

88.5
Cathy Beard
Arizona, 1993
Beard Creative Design
Symbol for Bobcat Films,
Video and Design.

88.6
Mark Fox
California, 1990
Black Dog
An editorial statement about
the business of graphic design, used
for self promotion.

89.1
Bob James
Ohio, 1993
Silver Moon Graphics
Symbol for WindCheetah, a
mirror system for bicycles.

89.2
Teri Klass
California, 1992
Klass Design/LA
Proposed mark for a
public relations firm.

89.3
Mark Fox
California, 1992
Black Dog
AD: Joel Fuller/Pinkhaus
Symbol for a Miami based
T-shirt company.

89.1

89.2

89.3

89

90.1

90.2

90.3

90.4

90.5

90.6

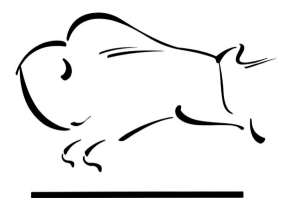

91.1

91.2

WOODMERE

91.3

90.1
Margo Chase
California, 1993
Margo Chase Design
Symbol/logo for an artists
resource directory.

90.2
Steve Liska
Illinois, 1987
Liska and Associates, Inc.
Illus: Bobbye Cochran
Symbol for an art deco
building complex.

90.3
Will Thompson
Tennessee, 1993
Thompson & Company
Symbol for Brazos Synthetic Leather.

90.4
Diana McKnight
Texas, 1992
Sibley/Peteet Design
Symbol for Lullaby Custom
Baby Linens and Clothing.

90.5
Rudiger Gotz
Minnesota, 1991
Duffy, Inc
AD: Joe Duffy/Rudiger Gotz
Illus: Rudiger Gotz/Lynn Schulte
Symbol for a line of men's
sportswear.

90.6
Tracy Holdeman
Kansas, 1992
Love Packaging Group
Symbol/logo for retail
dairy products.

91.1
Sheldon Lewis
California, 1992
Phippen Design Group
AD: Bonnie Phippen
Symbol for Buffalo Thunder, a shop
selling native American art.

91.2
John Evans
Texas, 1991
John Evans Design
Symbol for a high school
reunion of the Berkner Rams.

91.3
Donna Lehner/Hugh Whyte
New Jersey, 1992
Lehner & Whyte
Symbol for a real estate developer.

92.1

92.4

92.2

92.5

92.3

92.6

93.1

93.2

93.3

92.1
Michael Schwab
California, 1990
Michael Schwab Design
Symbol for a bicycle product line.

92.2
Wenping Hsiao
California, 1993
United Design
Symbol for a computer mouse-
Space Mouse.

92.3
Michael McGinn
New York, 1990
M Plus M Incorporated
AD: Michael McGinn/
Takai Matsumoto
Symbol for a land preservation
organization.

92.4
Sharon Werner
Minnesota, 1992
Duffy, Inc.
Symbol for a paper company.

92.5
Mark Fox
California, 1993
Black Dog
AD: Joanne Hoffman/Dennis McLeod
Symbol to illustrate an article on
thermal wax printers.

92.6
Luis Fitch
Ohio, 1990
Luis Fitch Diseño
Symbol/logo for a manufacturer
of apparel for little girls.

93.1
Scott Ray
Texas, 1992
Peterson & Company
Logo for the Dallas Zoological
Society Annual Report.

93.2
Mia Van Eimeren
California, 1992
Van Eimeren Design
Logo/symbol for a magazine
and television show.

93.3
Kevin Akers
California, 1990
Burson-Marsteller
Symbol for an ecological
organization.

HIDEAR

94

94.2

94.1
Craig Yamashita
California, 1992
See Why Design
Symbol for triathlon sportswear.

94.2
Michael Schwab
California, 1993
Michael Schwab Design
AD: Ruthie Sakheim
Symbol for cruise ship sports program.

95.1
John Alfred
Delaware, 1993
Delmarva Power Visual
Communications
AD: Christy MacIntyre
Symbol for a fish replenishment
program.

95.2
Michael MacIntyre
California, 1993
Symbol for international ocean
awareness and clean up.

95.3
Takaaki Matsumoto
New York, 1990
M Plus M Incorporated
AD: Takaaki Matsumoto/
Michael McGinn
Symbol for the Okinawa Aquarium.

95.4
Kim Tomlinson/Rick Tharp
California, 1991
Tharp Did It
Symbol for a manufacturer
of boat propellers.

95.5
Teri Klass
California, 1993
Klass Design/LA
Agency: The Waylon Company
Promotional symbol for a liqueur.

95.6
John Evans
Texas, 1993
Sibley/Peteet Design
Symbol for the Turtle Creek Run.

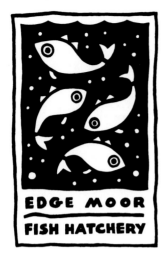

95.1

95.4

OCEAN AID

95.2

95.5

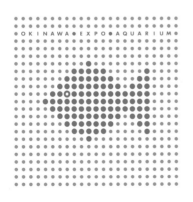

●OKINAWA●EXPO●AQUARIUM●

95.3

95.6

96.1

96

96.2

96.3

SMITHSONIAN MIGRATORY BIRD CENTER

96.4

GO-GO POLLO

96.5

96.6

97.1

PIZZAROTI

97.2

97.3

96.1
Ken Loh
California, 1992
Evenson Design Group
AD: Stan Evenson
Proposed symbol for Learning
Concepts Group.

96.2
Mark Fox
California, 1992
Black Dog
AD: Neal Sellman
Agency: Foote Cone & Belding
Symbol for a fast food promotion,
Taco Bell Night Owl.

96.3
Ken Koester
Texas, 1992
Brainstorm, Inc.
Symbol for The Shores, a
residential community.

96.4
Maria Biernik
Virginia, 1991
Crabtree & Jemison, Inc.
Symbol for a study project.

96.5 - 96.6
Marc Debartolomeis
New Jersey, 1992
Spot Design
Symbol for a take-out
restaurant chain.

97.1
Doug Powell
Georgia, 1992
Symbol/logo for a non-profit
building project.

97.2
Craig Yamashita
California, 1993
See Why Design
Logo/symbol for a restaurant.

97.3
Rodney Davidson
Alabama, 1992
Dogstar Design & Illustration
Symbol for a singer/pianist.

98.4

98

T H E   C A F E

98.1

98.5

CITY   **CITY**

98.2   98.3

98.6

98.1
Mauricio Arias
California, 1993
Arias Associates
Symbol/logo for a restaurant.

98.2 - 98.3
Steve Samiof
California, 1990
AD:MarySue Milliken/Susan Feiniger
Logo and Easter promotional logo
for a restaurant.

98.4
John Sayles
Iowa, 1993
Sayles Graphic Design
Logo for an umbrella
food service operation.

98.5
Michael Todd Lott
Ohio, 1992
Introspective Design
Symbol for a chef/cooking teacher

98.6
Bruce Yelaska
California, 1992
Bruce Yelaska Design
Symbol for Stacks', a
breakfast restaurant.

99.1
Sarah Huie
Georgia, 1990
Copeland Hirthler
Design & Communications
Logo for a casual restaurant.

99.2
John Sayles
Iowa, 1991
Sayles Graphic Design
Logo/symbol for a fast food service.

99.3
Tracy Holdeman
Kansas, 1993
Love Packaging Group
Symbol for a specialty coffee retailer.

99.1

99.2

99.3

100.1

100.2

100.3

100.4

100.1
John Sayles
Iowa, 1992
Sayles Graphic Design
Symbol for a coffeehouse.

100.2
Steven Guarnaccia
New York, 1992
Louise Fili Ltd.
AD: Louise Fili
Symbol for a restaurant.

100.3
Lee Perrault/George Holt
New Hampshire, 1993
Via Design Inc.
Symbol for a coffeehouse,

100.4
Woodie Pirtle
New York, 1992
Pentagram
AD: Michael Bierut
Symbol for The Good Diner
"A cup of coffee elevated
to sainthood."

101.1
Sharon K. Hanley
Washington, 1992
S.K. Hanley Design
Promotional logo for the
Oregon Dairy Council.

101.2
Gary Hudson
Massachusetts, 1993
G. Hudson Design
Symbol/logo for a
businessman's dining club.

101.3
Christine Nasser
California, 1990
Christine Nasser Design
& Illustration
Symbol for "Lets' Do Lunch"
a restaurant directory.

101.4
Gerald Bergstrom
Nebraska, 1993
David & Associates
AD: Randy Mattley, Barry Keller
Logo/symbol for a citywide
celebration.

101.5
Joe Duffy
Minnesota, 1993
Duffy, Inc
AD: Neil Powell/Joe Duffy
Symbol for Northwest Airline
Food Service.

101.6
Kristin Breslin Sommese
Pennsylvania, 1988
Sommese Design
Illus: Lanny Sommese
Symbol for a college pub.

100

101.1

101.2

101.3

FLAVOR
OF THE
FOURTH

101.4

101.5

101.6

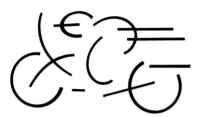

102.1

102.2

102.3

102.1
Kevin Akers
California, 1992
Burson-Marsteller
Symbol for a motorcycle grand prix.

102.2
Mark Fox
California, 1993
Black Dog
Motoman symbol for a clothing
manufacturer, man as machine and
vice versa.

102.3
Richard Cassis
Illinois, 1992
SPARC
Symbol for a bicycle shop in the
heart of the city.

103.1
John Evans
Texas, 1991
Sibley/Peteet Design
Symbol for a marathon.

103.2
Phill Thill
Wisconsin, 1992
Phill Thill Design
Illus: Ben Neff
Symbol for a medical equipment
manufacturers sales contest.

103.3
Jim Lange
Illinois, 1989
Jim Lange Design
AD: Jan Caille
Promotional symbol for
an obstacle race.

103.4
Bill Gardner/Sonia Greteman
Kansas, 1991
Gardner + Greteman
Symbol for Advantage Wichita,
a professional tennis team.

103.1

O • H • M • E • D • A

TRIATHLON

103.2

GATORADE
CROSS COUNTRY STEEPLE CHASE

103.3

103.4

104

104.1

104.2

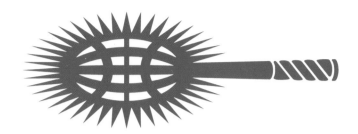

104.1
John Evans
Texas, 1989
Sibley/Peteet Design
Symbol for Sweatyme,
sportswear accessories.

104.2
Bruce Cocker
Massachusetts, 1993
Illus: Lee Busch
Symbol for National Sports
Center for the Disabled.

105.1
Jeff Weithman
Oregon, 1992
Nike Design
Illus: Lena James
Symbol for an international
tennis exhibition.

105.2
Kevin Flatt
Texas, 1993
Swieter Design
AD: John Swieter
Logo for a basketball line.

105.3
Rick Jackson
California, 1993
Rick Jackson & Associates
Logo for indoor golf.

105.1

105.2

Indoor
Golf
Center

105.3

106.1
Mamoru Shimokochi
California, 1991
Shimokochi/Reeves
Logo for a soccer team.

107.1
Scott Mires
California, 1993
Mires Design, Inc.
Illus: Tracy Sabin
Logo for a sport apparel company.

107.2
Katherine Lam
California, 1990
Patrick SooHoo Designers
AD: Patrick SooHoo
Symbol for an advertising
golf association.

107.3
Alan Colvin/Toki Wolf
Oregon, 1993
Nike Design
Illus: Suzie McClelland
Symbol for off-season football
training footwear.

107.4
Mike Quon/E. Kinneary
New York, 1992
Mike Quon Design Office
Symbol for special bike racing
championships.

106.1

107.3

107.1

107.4

107.2

108.1

108.2

108.1
Maureen Erbe
California, 1992
Maureen Erbe Design
Symbol for public concerts.

108.2
Rodney Davidson
Alabama,1993
Dogstar Design
Symbol for a piano technician.

109.1
David S. Rheinhardt
New Jersey, 1993
DSR Design
Logo for Michael Holland,
a musician.

109.2
Fred Anderson
Massachusetts, 1993
Groppi Design
Symbol for a music store/kennel.

109.3
Ellen Shapiro
New York, 1991
Shapiro Design Associates
Illus: Alexander Acker
Symbol for a musician.

109

109.1

MUTT HOUSE MUSIC

109.2

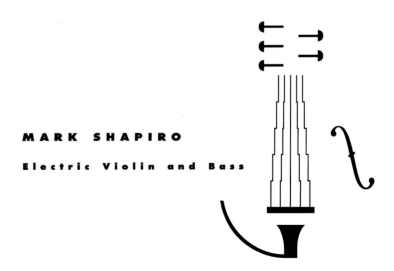

MARK SHAPIRO

Electric Violin and Bass

109.3

110

110.1

110.2

P I L L A R

110.3

110.1
Michael Schwab
California, 1993
Michael Schwab Design
AD: Jeff Potter
Symbol for an investment
banking firm.

110.2
Julie Tsuchiya
California, 1992
Tsuchiya Sloneker Communication
Proposed logo for a hotels'
tenth anniversary.

110.3
Steve Tolleson
California, 1991
Tolleson Design
Symbol/logo for the Pillar Corp.

111.1
James A. Stygar
Virginia, 1992
Stygar Group, Inc.
Symbol for an association
of businesses.

111.2
John Alfred
Delaware, 1992
Delmarva Power Visual
Communications
AD: Christy MacIntyre
Illus: Wayne Parmenter
Symbol for a library support group.

111.3
Doug Zimmerman
Iowa, 1993
Younkers, Inc.
Symbol for a restaurant in
a department store.

111.1

Friends of the
Wilmington Library

111.2

THE TEA ROOM

111.3

112.1

112.2

112.3

112.1
Scott W. Santoro
New York, 1989
Worksight
Logo for Gotham Fine Arts Gallery.

112.2
Art Chantry
Washington, 1991
Art Chantry Designs
Symbol for Estrus Records.

112.3
Bill Gardner/Sonia Greteman
Kansas, 1991
Gardner + Greteman
Symbol for Wichita Center
for the Arts.

113.1
Mark Anderson
Missouri, 1993
Eilts Anderson Tracy
Symbol for an Ozark Mountains
real estate development company.

113.2
John Alfred
Delaware, 1993
Delmarva Power Visual
Communication
AD: Christy MacIntyre
Symbol to promote small business
and economic growth.

113.3
Joel Tachau
Illinois, 1993
Monogram Design, Inc.
AD: Scott Markman
Symbol for an organization which
teaches cultural heritage, while pro-
viding exposure to architecture.
Their goal is to assume ownership of
damaged buildings and restore them.

113.4
Becca Bootes
California, 1992
Bootes Design
Symbol for a film production company.

113.5
Brian Burns
Virginia 1992
The Martin Agency
Symbol for a chamber of
commerce project.

113.6
Michael Bierut/Dorit Len
New York, 1992
Pentagram Design
Logo for Gotham Equities, a New
York real estate development firm.

UPTOWN CORPORATION

113.1

NEW CASTLE COUNTY CHAMBER OF COMMERCE

113.2

YOUNG URBAN PRESERVATIONISTS SOCIETY

113.3

WINDY CITY

PRODUCTIONS

113.4

INTERCITY VISIT

113.5

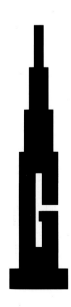

113.6

114.1
Mark Fox
California, 1992
Black Dog
AD: Kay Crowson/
Noble & Associates
Symbol for a school program
to promote drinking milk.

114.2
Scott Ray
Texas, 1993
Peterson & Company
Symbol for the Jewish Home
Lecture Organization.

114.3
James A. Stygar
Virginia, 1992
Stygar Group, Inc.
Symbol for Southern Cross Builders.

115.1
Bill Gardner/Sonia Greteman
Kansas, 1993
Gardner + Greteman
Symbol for Pechin Construction Co.

115.2
Maureen Erbe
California, 1992
Maureen Erbe Designs
Symbol for the city of Santa Ana.

115.3
Ken Loh
California, 1992
Evenson Design Group
AD: Stan Evenson
Proposed symbol for Learning
Concepts Group.

115.4
Tricia Rauen
California, 1992
Evenson Design Group
AD: Stan Evenson
Proposed symbol for Learning
Concepts Group.

115.5
Art Chantry
Washington, 1991
Art Chantry Designs
Symbol for a silk screen printer.

115.6
William Mo
California, 1993
Symbol/logo for a software package
for plant automation systems.

114.1

114.2

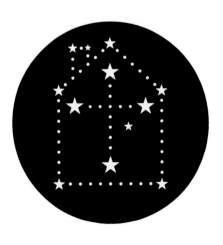

114.3

115.1

115.2

115.3

115.4

POST·INDUSTRIAL PRESS

115.5

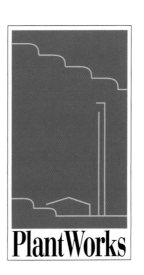

PlantWorks

115.6

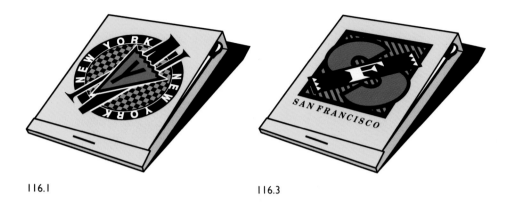

116.1

116.3

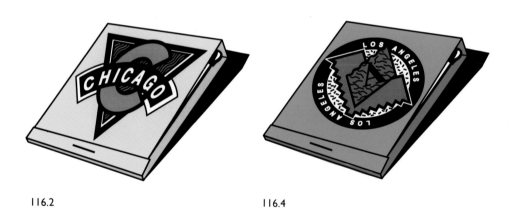

116.2

116.4

116.5

16.1-116.4
Mamoru Shimokochi
California, 1991
Shimokochi/Reeves
AD: Mamoru Shimokochi/
Anne Reeves
Illus: Mamoru Shimokochi/
Tracy McGoldrick
Symbols for design directories.

117.1
Tricia Rauen
California, 1993
Evenson Design Group
AD: Stan Evenson
Proposed symbol for Learning
Concepts Group.

117.2
Kevin Akers
California, 1993
Design With Personality
Symbol for Ink-Well, a
printing broker.

117.3
Mark Fox
California, 1993
Black Dog
Symbol for a clothing manufacturer.

117.1

117.2

117.3

118.1

118.2

118.3

118.1
Bob Cosgrove
Illinois, 1988
Liska and Associates, Inc.
AD: Steve Liska
Symbol for a conference on human interaction with computers.

118.2
Sharon Werner
Minnesota, 1992
Werner Design Werks, Inc.
Symbol for a design studio.

118.3
Tracy Holdeman
Kansas, 1993
Love Packaging Group
AD: Tracy Holdeman/Robert Elliot
Symbol for a firm that specializes in faux finishes.

119.1
Alan Morris
New Jersey, 1992
Morris Design
Symbol for a graphic design studio.

119.2
Mike Quon
New York, 1992
Mike Quon Design Office
AD: Scott Fishoff
Symbol for a "back to school" promotion.

119.3
Patty O'Leary
New Hampshire, 1992
Via Design, Inc.
AD: Lee Perrault
Symbol for a copywriter.

119.4-119.6
Jeffrey Dever/Douglas Dunbebin
Maryland, 1992/93
Dever Designs, Inc.
Promotional logos for a graphic design studio.

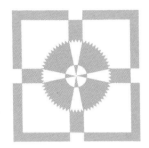

119.1

119.4

119.2

119.5

119.3

119.6

WRITERS ON WRITING

120.1

PROOFREADING CHECK-UP

120.5

SELF-SURVEY

120.9

CONFERENCING STRATEGIES

120.2

PARTNER TALK

120.6

WRITE ANGLE

120.10

FAST FOCUS

120.3

WHAT'S THE POINT?

120.7

PLANNING STRATEGY

120.11

DID YOU NOTICE?

120.4

FOR MORE HELP

120.8

SELF-CHECK

120.12

REVISING STRATEGIES

121.1

WRITERS' GALLERY

121.2

CRITICAL THINKING

121.3

READ TO WRITE

121.4

MAKE CONNECTIONS

121.5

121.6

120.1-121.6
John Nishimoto
New York, 1991
Carbone Smolan Associates
AD: Beth Bangor/Leslie Smolan
Program of icons for an
eductional series on writing
created for a publisher.

122.1

Truckin' Time

122.2

122.3

122.1
Ron Kellum
New York, 1990
Ron Kellum, Inc.
Symbol for Unherd of Productions.

122.2
Wendy Behrens
Illinois, 1992
Simantel Group
AD: Susie Ketterer
Symbol for a TV program on
the trucking industry.

122.3
Christina Freyss/Peter Harrison
New York, 1992
Pentagram Design
Illus: David Suter
Symbol for a computer
consulting company.

123.1
Dean Van Eimeren
California, 1992
Saatchi & Saatchi DFS/Pacific
Logo for a library.

123.2
José Bila Rodriguez/Bill Reuter
California, 1991
William Reuter Design
AD: Bill Reuter
Symbol for a book signing event.

123.3
Supon Phornirunlit/Dave E. Prescott
Washington, D.C., 1993
Supon Design Group
AD: Supon Phornirunlit
Symbol for a book packager.

123.4
John Norman
Oregon, 1993
Nike Design
Illus: Lena James
Symbol for house stock photography
and illustration department.

123.5
Richard Boynton
Virginia, 1993
Boynton Design
Symbol for a copywriter,
indicating traditional fund-
amentals and technology.

 LOS ANGELES
PUBLIC LIBRARY

123.1

123.2

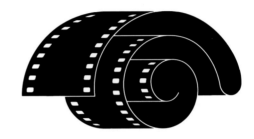

123.4

123.3

123.5

124.1
Susan Hochbaum
New York, 1992
Pentagram
Illus: Rolla Herman
Logo for Atomics Ironworks, manu-
facturers of iron home accessories.

124.2
Michael Carr
Illinois, 1992
Michael Carr Design
Symbol for KaBoom, a dance club.

125.1
Michael Carr
Illinois, 1993
Michael Carr Design
Logo for a neighborhood restaurant,
"a great place to hang your hat".

125.2
David Lemley
Washington, 1992
David Lemley Design
AD: Robert Raible/Kevin Gardiner
Symbol for the kitchen department
in a department store.

125.3
Peter Horjus
California, 1993
Horjus Design
Symbol for Byron Pepper
Photography.

125.4
Wendy Behrens
Illinois, 1991
Wendy Behrens Design
Symbol for a birthing center.

125.5
Kimberly Baer
California, 1993
Kimberly Baer Design
Logo/symbol for a record company.

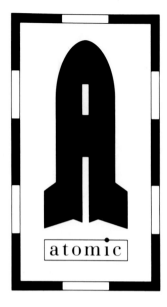

124.1

124.2

125.1

125.4

125.2

PUMP
RECORDS

125.5

125.3

126.1

126.2

126.1
James Cross
California, 1992
Siegel & Gale/Cross
Symbol for Ideas '92, the triangle has
an idea. It either wants to be a
french curve or is in love with one.

126.2
Scott W. Santoro
New York, 1989
Worksight
For a graphic design studio, channels
or connecting links - plumbing parts
are used as the theme in studio
promotions.

127.1
Rick Jackson
California, 1993
Rick Jackson & Associates
Logo/symbol for a men's
accessories manufacturer.

127.2
John Heiden
California, 1989
John Heiden Design
Symbol for Book Soup, it represents
an abstraction of the store name.

127.3
Gary Clare
New York, 1993
Javier Romero Design Group
AD: Javier Romero
Symbol for "Shout", a studio
self-promotion.

127.4
Dan Flynn
New Mexico, 1993
Vaughn Wedeen Creative
Symbol for a healthcare organization.

127.5
Mark Fox
California, 1989
Black Dog
AD: Clay Doyle
Agency:Clay Doyle Design Group
Symbol for UCLA Medical Center.

127.6
Michael Bierut/Esther Bridausky
New York, 1993
Pentagram Design
Logo for a trade organization.

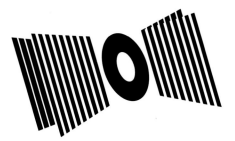

HOLLYVOGUE *Neckwear*

127.1

NIPSI

127.4

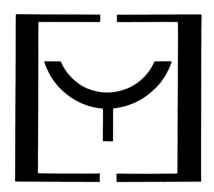

127.2

127.5

127.3

THE
FASHION
CENTER

127.6

128.1

128.6

128.4

128.2

128.7

128.5

128.3

128.8

Cornucopia

129.1

129.2

129.3

128.1-128.8
Jon Flaming
Texas, 1993
Jon Flaming Design
Identities for different
departments for Neiman-Marcus'
Christmas promotion.

129.1
Mary Scott
California,1993
Maddocks & Company
Logo for a furniture store.

129.2
Mauricio Arias/Catherine Richards
California, 1993
Arias Associates
Symbol for a hotel, Shutters.

129.3
Neil Powell
Minnesota, 1992
Duffy, Inc.
AD: Joe Duffy/Neil Powell
Logo for Weiland Furniture.

130.1

130.2

130.3

130.1
John Evans
Texas, 1991
Sibley/Peteet Design
Symbol for Spirit Cruises, a festive
dinner/sightseeing harbor cruise.

130.2
Rudiger Gotz
Minnesota, 1991
Duffy, Inc.
AD: Sharon Werner/
Todd Waterbury
Illus: Rudiger Gotz/Lynn Schulte
Logo for a rough terrain bicycle.

130.3
Haley Johnson
Minnesota, 1990
Charles S. Anderson Design Co.
AD: Charles S. Anderson
Illus: Randal Dahlk/Haley Johnson
Logo for a watch company
with global appeal.

131.1
Nancy Edmonds
California, 1993
Edmonds Graphics
Logo for an auto mechanic.

131.2
Julie Tsuchiya
California, 1991
Tsuchiya Slonecker
Commmunications
Symbol for Shipman Moving Co.

131.3
Tracy Holdeman
Kansas, 1992
Love Pacakaging Group
Symbol for an in-house trucking fleet.

131.4
Dan Slavin
Illinois, 1989
Slavin Associates
Symbol for American LeisuRail, who
provides trains to special events.

131.5
John Sayles
Iowa, 1991
Sayles Graphic Design
Logo is a pun on the business name.

KEEFE AUTOMOTIVE

131.1

131.2

131.4

131.3

LOGO-MOTIVE

TEXTILE SCREEN PRINTING
AND SPECIALTY ADVERTISING

131.5

132.1

DESKTALK

132.2

132.3

133.1

133.2

132.1
Mike Schmalz
Iowa, 1993
McCullough Graphics
AD: Jeff MacFarlane
Symbol for Dubuque Area Chamber
of Commerce - the key to the city

132.2
Robert Louey
California, 1992
Louey-Rubino Design Group
Logo for an electronic office system.

132.3
Sharon Werner
Minnesota, 1992
Werner design Werks Inc.
Logo for a contract furniture business.

133.1
Mark Fox
California, 1993
Black Dog
Promotional symbol for a table
design at a museum fundraiser.
The skull and crosstools illustrates
 a Russion Constructivist quote -
"Death to Art!"

133.2
John Sayles
Iowa, 1991
Sayles Graphic Design
Logo for a church youth organization.

134.1

134.2

134.1
Dan Simon
California, 1992
The Mednick Group
AD: Scott Mednick/Dan Simon
Logo for an elite fitness organization.

134.2
Denise Vorhees
California, 1992
Abrams Design Group
AD: Colleen Abrams
Logo for a software company.

135.1
Dan Simon/John Smeaton
California, 1992
The Mednick Group
AD: Dan Simon/Scott Mednick
Logo for an ad campaign.

135.2
Stephen Sieler
California, 1990
Stephen Sieler Design
Symbol for a conference on man-
ufacturing - The Global Factory.

135.3
John Norman
Oregon, 1991
Nike Design
Promotional logo for a basketball tour.

135.4
Edward Walter
New York, 1991
Edward Walter Design, Inc
Illus: Jack Mortensbak
Symbol for a real estate development
catering to the international fashion
and textile industries.

135.5
Lynell Wilcha
Pennsylvania, 1990
Lynell Wicha Design
Logo for an events/party
planning organization.

135.1

135.4

135.2

135.5

135.3

136.1

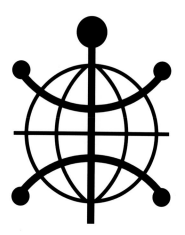

136.2

136.3

136.1
Jon Flaming
Texas, 1993
Jon Flaming Design
Symbol for CircuitMan, a clothing line.

136.2
Mark Fox
California, 1992
Black Dog
AD: John Liegey
Agency: Chiat Day Mojo
Rejected symbol for Planet Reebok.

136.3
Rick Yurk
California, 1993
James Robie Design Associates
AD: James Robie
Logo for lightweight guidebooks.

137.1
Greg Morgan
Texas, 1993
Joseph Rattan Design
AD: Joe Rattan
Symbol for Habitat World, an organiza-
tion that builds homes for the homeless.

137.2
Cameron Woo
California, 1990
AT & T Graphics Group
AD: John Seminerio
Symbol for a conference on African art.

137.3
Bill Gardner/Sonia Greteman/James
Strange
Kansas, 1993
Gardner + Greteman
Symbol for Earth Day.

137.4
Bill Gardner/Sonia Greteman
Kansas, 1992
Gardner + Greteman
Symbol for Green Horizons,
an environmental store.

137.5
Jeanne Simonian
California, 1993
Silicon Graphic Creative
AD: Frank Doyle
Symbol for a seminar on visual
computing systems, servers
and super computers.

137.1

137.4

137.2

137.5

137.3

138.1

138.2

138.3

Community Partnership
of Santa Clara County

138.4

138.5

LAKEMARY
CENTER

138.6

138.1
Michael Stinson
California, 1993
Stinson Design
Symbol for a community police orga-
nization against drugs and violence.

138.2
Matt DeFrain/Richard Cassis
Illinois, 1993
SPARC
Symbol for employee courses.

138.3
Teri Klass
California, 1992
AD: Jane Beard/Sharon Sato
Symbol for a Women in
Design conference.

138.4
Earl Gee/Fani Chung
California, 1992
Earl Gee Design
Symbol for an organization which
promotes healthy communities.

138.5
Wendy Behrens
Illinois, 1993
Wendy Behrens Design
Symbol for a preschool.

138.6
Patrice Eilts
Missouri, 1993
Eilts Anderson Tracy
Logo for a center for the mentally
or physically disabled.

139.1
Ronn Campisi
Massachusetts, 1987
Ronn Campisi Design
Illus: Patrick Blackwell
Symbol for the Christmas edition of
the Boston Globe magazine.

139

139.1

140.1

STARS

OAKVILLE
CAFE

140.2

Atlanta
1996

140.4

140.3

140.1
Bill Gardner/Sonia Greteman
Kansas, 1991
Gardner + Greteman
Symbol for a travel agency.

140.2
Debra Nichols/Roxanne Malek
California, 1993
Debra Nichols Design
Logo for a restaurant.

140.3
Kimberly Baer
California, 1992
Kimberly Baer Design
Symbol for StarBase, a software program.

140.4
Brad Copeland
Georgia, 1988
Copeland Hirthler
Design Communications
Symbol created for Atlanta's bid
for the Olympics.

141.1
Kevin Akers
California, 1991
Design With Personality
Symbol for StarSpot, theatre lighting.

141.2
Don Kline
New York, 1987
Siegel & Gale, New York
Symbol for 24 hour banking.

141.3
James A. Stygar
Virginia, 1992
Stygar Group, Inc
Logo for a manufacturer
of cooking apparel.

141.1

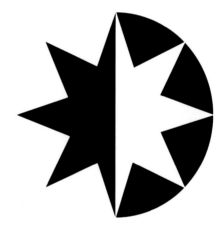

141.2

141.3

142.1

142.2

142.3

142.1
David Reneric/John O'Brien
California, 1989
Cimarron/Bacon/O'Brien
AD:Jeffrey Bacon/John O'Brien
Design studio logo, the letter "C"
for Cimarron evolving into a star
for Hollywood.

142.2
Douglas Bogner
California, 1993
Bullzye Design & Marketing
Symbol for a television channel.

142.3
Bill Gardner/Sonia Greteman
Kansas, 1993
Gardner + Greteman
Symbol for Planet Hair, a salon.

143.1
Matt Lynaugh/Gloria Lee
Texas, 1992
Buds Design Kitchen
Logo for a science radio program.

143.2
Mamoru Shimokochi
California, 1992
Shimokochi/Reeves
AD: Mamoru Shimokochi/Anne Reeves
Logo for a print production company.

143.3
Traci Daberko
Washington, 1993
The Leonhardt Group
Symbol for a concert promotion.

143.4
Richard Cassis
Illinois, 1992
SPARC
Symbol for a theatre group aimed
at raising funds by selling blocks of
tickets to corporate sponsors.

143.5
Richard Cassis
Illlinois, 1993
SPARC
AD: Richard Cassis/Marc Miller
Symbol for an eyeglass broker.

Earth & Sky

143.1

143.4

SKYAD

143.2

MOON

MILLER'S ORIGINAL OPTICAL NETWORK INC

143.5

US WEST CELLULAR STARLINE CONCERT SERIES

143.3

144.1

144.2

I-DEAS™

144.3

144.1
Kirsten Wiechert
Kansas, 1991
BTDesign
AD: Carey Treanor
Symbol for Environmental
Management Resources, Inc.

144.2
Katja Burkett
Georgia, 1993
Gill Design
AD: Martha Gill
Symbol for Moonlight Advertising.

144.3
Eric Rickabaugh
Ohio, 1992
Rickabaugh Graphics
Illus: Tony Meuser
Proposed logo for a 3-D
modeling software program.

145.1
Bruce Edwards
Minnesota, 1991
Rapp Collins Communications
Symbol for a hair salon
with tanning booths.

145.2
Scott Feldmann
Florida, 1991
Magic Pencil
Logo for the Creative Club of Orlando.

145.3
Mark Fox
California, 1987
Black Dog
A personal political statement in the
form of a pro-solar power logo.

145.4
Michael Stinson
California, 1993
Stinson Design
Symbol for SpectraSign - a
complete sign service.

145.5
John Coy, Albert Choi
California, 1993
COY, Los Angeles
Logo for a TV commercial
production company.

145.1

145.3

145.2

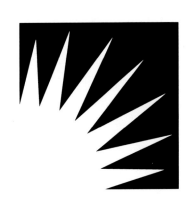

145.4

145.5

146.1

146.3

AFTER THE
FLOOD

146.2

146.4

ON THE EDGE

146.5

148.1
John Alfred
Delaware, 1993
Delmarva Power Visual
Communications
Logo for company sponsored event
to clean up beaches and waterways.

148.2
Bruce Edwards
Minnesota, 1990
John Ryan Co.
Illus: Anthony Russo
Symbol for rugged mens wear.

148.3
Anne Vetter
Colorado, 1993
Bob Coonts Design Group
AD: Bob Coonts
Symbol for Homefest, a furniture
and interior design company.

148.4
Bill Gardner/Sonia Greteman
Kansas, 1991
Gardner + Greteman
Logo/symbol for a community
celebration.

149.1
Nadine Flowers
Massachusetts, 1992
Barrett Design Inc.
Symbol for a manufacturer
of robotic arms.

149.2
Mark Oldach
Illinois, 1989
Mark Oldach Design
Logo for a graphic designer.

149.3
John Norman
Oregon, 1992
Nike Design
Illus: David Gill
Logo/symbol for a shoe.

149.1

149

149.2

149.3

150.1

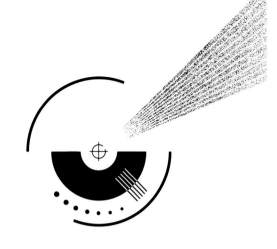

150.4

150.2

CROSSROADS

RECORDS

150.5

PACIFIC
DESIGN
CENTER

X rev

150.6

150.3

150.1
Mark T. Selfe/Kit Hinrichs
California, 1992
Pentagram
Logo that suggests "design is the cen-
ter of everything" for a structure that
houses more than 200 showrooms.

150.2
Robin Perkins/Jeff Breidenbach/
Robert Merk
Massachusetts, 1993
Clifford Selbert Design
Logo for a new bicycle wheel.

150.3
Mark Fox
California, 1989
Black Dog
AD: Mary Ann Dibs
Logo for recording artists,
Club Nouveau.

150.4
Paula Wong/Mary Hubert
Washington, 1989
Aldus Creative Services
Symbol for imaging and
service bureaus.

150.5
Douglas Dunbebin/Jeffrey L. Dever
Maryland, 1991
Dever Designs Inc.
Logo which shows that discs, CD or
tape have an impact on the world.

150.6
Kevin Akers
California, 1988
Design With Personality
Symbol for BioTherm, a greenhouse
heating company.

151.1
David Kampa
Texas, 1990
Fuller Dyal & Stamper
AD: Mary Conrad Castagna
Symbol for an Association
of Heart Surgeons.

151.2
Debra Nichols/Kelan Smith
California, 1991
Debra Nichols Design
Symbol for Gas Company tower.

151.3
John Norman
Oregon, 1992
Nike Design
AD: John Norman/David Kennedy
Agency: Weiden & Kennedy
Symbol for the American Indian
College Fund.

151.1

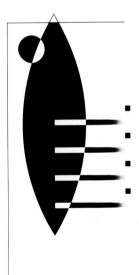

151.2

151.3

152.1

152.2

RED CROSS MASS CARE VOLUNTEER 10.89 THE CITY

152.3

152.4

152.1
Phill Thill
Wisconsin, 1992
Phill Thill Design
Logo for snap-on tools.

152.2
John Coy/Sean Alatorre
California, 1993
COY, Los Angeles
Logo for a sandwich shop.

152.3
Mark Fox
California, 1989
Black Dog
Symbol for Red Cross Earthquake Relief
following the San Francisco quake.

152.4
Paula Scher
New York, 1987
Pentagram
Logo for the School of Visual Arts.

153.1
Holly Copus Hagen
Maryland, 1992
Dever Designs Inc.
AD: Jeffrey L. Dever
Logo for a preschool math program.

153.2
Stewart Monderer
Massachusetts, 1993
Stewart Monderer Design, Inc.
Logo for a restaurant.

153.3
Ross Rezac/Martin Skoro
Minnesota, 1989
Martin Ross Design
Symbol for Vision of Success,
career consultants.

153.4
Dan McNulty
California, 1993
McNulty & Company
Logo for a special event planner.

153.5
David Levy
Georgia, 1993
Levy Design Inc.
Logo for a graphic design firm.

153.6
Bruce Johnson
New York, 1991
Iroquois Image Works
AD: Jake Jacobi
Logo for a graphic design studio.

153.1

153.4

153.2

153.5

153.3

153.6

154.1

154.1
Christine Dashner
California, 1992
Visual Asylum
AD: MaeLin & Amy Levine
Logo for a sandal manufacturer.

154.2
John Sayles
Iowa, 1991
Sayles Graphic Design
Logo for a humanitarian award.

154.3
Jeffrey L. Dever
Maryland, 1990
Dever Designs Inc.
Symbol for. Reach, an organization
promoting child health in
developing countries.

155.1
Sharon Werner
Minnesota, 1990
Duffy, Inc.
Illus: Sharon Werner/Lynn Schulte
A Logo for a paper company's
recycling program.

154.2

154.3

155.1

156.1

156.2

156.3

156.1
Mike Schmalz
Iowa, 1991
McCullough Graphics
Logo for Arlux Fiber Optics.

156.2
Mark Scott Carroll
Missouri, 1990
Siren Design
Logo for the St. Louis Regional
Arts Commission.

156.3
Michael Strassburger
Washington, 1992
Modern Dog
AD: Michael Strassburger/
Scott St. John
Logo for a teenage game show.

157.1
Jennifer Morla
California, 1988
Morla Design
Logo for a photographer.

157.2
Frank Ford
Louisiana, 1992
FrankForDesign
Logo for a software developer.

157.3
William Homan
Minnesota, 1991
William Homan Design
Logo for a support organization
for inner city schools.

157.4
Kevin Whaley
Minnesota, 1991
GrapndPré & Whaley, Ltd.
Logo for an offset printer.

157.5
Richard Cassis
Illinois, 1991
SPARC
Logo for SPARC, a design firm.

157.6
Scott Greer
Utah, 1993
University of Utah Division of
Continuing Education
Logo for the Communication
Institute at the University of Utah.

157.1

157.4

157.2

157.5

THE CITY

157.3

157.6

158.1

158.1
Lanny Sommese
Pennsylvania, 1992
Sommese Design
Logo for Design Mirage, a design studio.

158.2
Edward Walter
New York, 1991
Edward Walter Design, Inc.
Illus: Edward Walter/
Jack Mortensbak
Logo for a product development firm.

158.3
John Evans
Texas, 1993
John Evans Design
Logo for John Evans Design.

159.1
Richard Nelson
Minnesota, 1993
Worrell Design
AD: Richard Nelson/Lisa Busch
Logo for an electrical contractor.

159.2
Jeff Weithman
Oregon, 1992
Nike Design
Illus: David Gill
Logo for Echelon, a line of cycling
footwear and apparel.

159.3
Dan Weeks
Ohio, 1993
Weeks & Associates
Logo for Exhibitry, an exhibit
services company.

159.4
Frank D'Astolfo
New York, 1990
Frank D'Asrolfo Design
Logo for Entrekin/Zucco Advertising Inc.

159.5
James Pettus
Connecticut, 1992
pure
Logo for a fashion retailer.

159.6
Jeffrey Moss
Arizona, 1990
J. W. Moss & Co.
Logo for Grafikhaus, a graphic design
firm. The G is meant to portray film
reels for the film department.

158.2

158.3

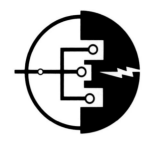

Ellingson Electric

159.1

159.4

159.2

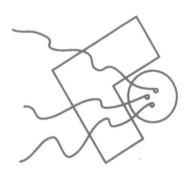

fabrique

159.5

159.3

haus

159.6

159

160.1

160.2

160.3

160.1
Michael Todd Lott
Ohio, 1993
Introspective Design
Logo for Galaxy, sales and
installation of satellite dishes.

160.2
David Collins
Virginia, 1993
Grafik Communications Ltd.
AD: Judy F. Kirpich
Logo for Grafik, a design firm.

160.3
Bradford Kear/Jerome Cloud
Pennsylvania, 1993
Cloud and Gehshan Assoc. Inc.
Logo for a environmental/graphic
design firm.

161.1
Thomas McNulty
California, 1993
Profile Design
AD: Kenichi Nishiwaki
Logo for Hamanaka Group.
a chain manufacturer.

161.2
Arnold Yew
Hawaii, 1993
Whodunit Design
Personal Logo for Mark Higgins a
designer of evening dresses.

161.3
Ken Shafer
Washington, 1991
Ken Shafer Design
Logo for HyperGrafix, a clothing line.

161.4
Michael Todd Lott
Ohio, 1991
Introspective Design
Logo for Holtel Construction Co.

161.5
John Heiden
California, 1984
John Heiden Design
Logo for John Heiden Design.

161.6
Nicholas Sinadinos/Scott Hardy
Illinois, 1993
Nicholas Associates
Logo for Illinois Theatrical, sellers of
dance and theatrical costumes.

161.1

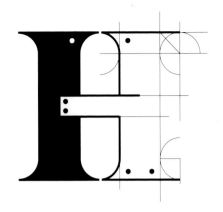

161.4

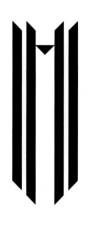

161.2

161.5

161.3

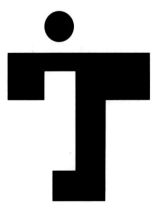

161.6

162.1

162.2

162.3

162.1
James A. Stygar
Virginia, 1988
Stygar Group, Inc.
Logo for Intermart, a trade center
for international business.

162.2
Nicholas Sinadinos
Illinois, 1993
Nicholas Associates
Logo for Krueger Design Group, a
retail interior design firm.

162.3
Bill Gardner/Sonia Greteman
Kansas, 1992
Gardner + Greteman
Logo/Acronym for Kansas Elk Training
Center for the Handicapped.

163.1
John Heiden
California, 1987
John Heiden Design
Personal mark for Linda Allen.

163.2
John Narimatsu
California, 1992
Kysar Narimatsu Associates
Logo for design consultants.

163.3
David Kampa
Texas, 1992
Kampa Design
Logo for Loophole Entertainment,
music industry management.

163.4
Gerry Rosentswieg
California, 1993
The Graphics Studio
Logo for Marks Realty.

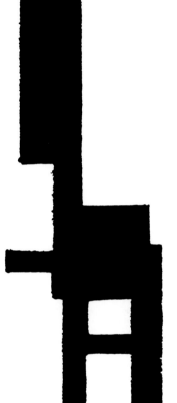

163.2

163.3

163.1

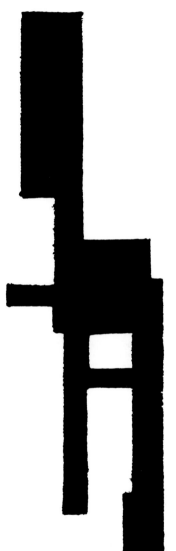

163.4

164.1

164.4

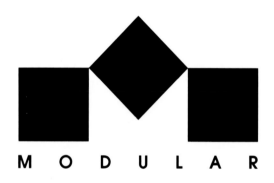

M O D U L A R

164.2

164.5

METROWEST

164.3

M O G U L S

164.6

165.1

165.2

165.3

164.1
James A. Stygar
Virginia, 1989
Stygar Group, Inc.
Logo for Micromagnetic, manufacturer
of custom computer disks.

164.2
Susan Merritt
California, 1988
CWA, Inc.
Illus: Susan Merritt/Jack Davis
Logo for a company that manufac-
tures temporary modular buildings.

164.3
Art Garcia
Texas, 1992
SullivanPerkins
AD: Art Garcia/Ron Sullivan
Logo for a landscape company.

164.4
Gerry Rosentswieg
California, 1993
The Graphics Studio
Personal mark for MeraLee Goldman.

164.5
Kathy Middleton
California, 1992
Pat Davis Design
AD: Pat Davis
Logo for Jack Metzen fine jewelry.

164.6
Richard Patterson
California, 1993
Sargent & Berman
AD: Greg Berman/Peter Sargent
Logo for a supper club.

165.1
Anonymous Graphics
California, 1992
Logo for Massini, a furniture
showroom.

165.2
Glenn Johnson
California, 1993
Jerry Takigawa Design
AD: Jerry Takigawa
Logo for Mark Watson
Building and Renovation.

165.3
Bill Gardner/Sonia Greteman/
James Strange
Kansas, 1993
Gardner + Greteman
Logo for Motorworks Auto Repair.

166.1

MICHAEL

166.2

166.3

166.1
Tracy Holdeman
Kansas, 1993
Love Packaging Group
Logo for Network Interface Corporation.

166.2
Jon Flaming
Texas, 1993
Jon Flaming Design
Logo for a filmmaker.

166.3
Charles S. Anderson/Daniel Olson
Minnesota, 1989
Charles S. Anderson Design Co.
Logo for a printer, suggesting the gear
that drives the cylinder of a press.

167.1
Rick Vaughn
New Mexico, 1992
Vaughn Wedeen Creative
Logo for photoplotters.

167.2
John Heiden
California, 1989
John Heiden Design
Logo for a youth
oriented music label.

167.3
David Kampa
Texas, 1992
Kampa Design
Logo for The Ruddy Group, a film
and video production company.

167.4
Bill Jones
Kentucky, 1992
Kirby Stephens Design Inc.
AD: Kirby Stephens
Logo for Sterling Imaging Inc., a
radiology firm. X-rays formed by
the "S" pass through the body "I".

167.5
Dan Weeks
Ohio, 1993
Weeks & Associates
Logo for the Toledo Symphony.

167.6
Richard Nelson
Minnesota, 1993
Worrell Design
Logo for a line of Rollerblades.

QC GRAPHICS

167.1

167.4

random

RECORDS

167.2

167.5

167.3

TARMAC

167.6

168.1

U N L I M I T E D, I N C.

168.2

168.1
Jerome Cloud
Pennsylvania, 1987
Cloud and Gehshan Assoc. Inc
Logo for T Squared Architects.

168.2
Denise K. Keefe
California, 1990
Klarquist Design
Logo for a digital photo retouching
and image manipulating firm.

169.1
Kevin Whaley
Minnesota, 1989
GrandPré & Whaley Ltd.
Logo for artist rep, Janet Virnig.

169.2
Bill Gardner/Sonia Greteman
Kansas, 1991
Gardner + Greteman
Logo for Wichita Technical School.

169.3
Robert Sirko
Indiana, 1992
R Sirko Design
Logo for Valparaiso University Alumni.

169.4
Rick Yurk
California, 1993
James Robie Design Associates
AD: James Robie
Logo for the employee benefits
program at an aerospace company.

169.1

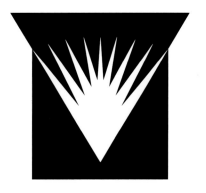

169.3

169.2

169.4

170.1

170.2

170.3

170.1
Kevin Akers
California, 1989
Design With Personality
Logo for Wilson Communications.

170.2
T.A. Hahn
New Jersey, 1992
T.A. Hahn Design
Agency: Wilson Creative Marketing
Logo for Wirth Florists.

170.3
Greg Clarke
California, 1991
Wiggly Man Design
Logo for WiseGeist, an
artists cooperative.

171.1
Greg Simpson
New York, 1990
Pushpin Group
Logo for Stephen Wilkes Photography.

171.2
Takaaki Matsumoto
New York, 1990
M Plus M Incorporated
AD: Takaaki Matsumoto/
Michael McGinn
Logo for Day Without Art.

171.3
Mark Fox
California, 1992
Black Dog
Logo for a photographer,
Will Mosgrove.

171.4
Alan Colvin
Oregon, 1991
Nike Design
AD: Alan Colvin/Ron Dumas
Illus: Alan Colvin/David Gill
Logo for cross training.

171.5
Kevin Flatt, Paul Munsterman,
John Swieter
Texas, 1993
Swieter Design
Logo for a basketball with a panel
for owner identification.

171.6
Frank D'Astolfo
New York, 1992
Frank D'Astolfo Design
Logo for XYZ Productions, a producer
of publications and radio programs.

171.1

171.4

171.2

171.5

171.3

171.6

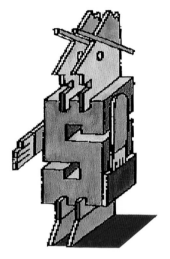

172.1

172.2

172.1
Art Garcia
Texas, 1990
SullivanPerkins
AD: Ron Sullivan/Art Garcia
Logo for the business side of design,
the SullivanPerkins Dollar Man.

172.2
Mike Holcomb
Oregon, 1993
Fine & Applied Art,
University of Oregon
Logo for a demonstration project,
combining design, business and com-
munications students.

173.1
Dan Weeks
Ohio, 1992
Weeks & Associates
Logo for an exhibit services
company, 2 Scale.

173.2
Kelly Allen
Texas, 1992
SullivanPerkins
AD: Ron Sullivan
Third anniversary logo for Meltzer
And Martin, a marketing firm.

173.3
Dan Richards
Texas, 1993
SullivanPerkins
AD: Ron Sullivan
Fourth anniversary logo
for Martin and Meltzer.

173.4
Ryoichi Yotsumoto
California, 1992
Laura Coe Design Associates
AD: Laura Coe Wright
Anniversary logo.

173.5
Tim Varnau
Illinois, 1992
Listenberger Design Associates
Logo for the office of the
Chapter 13 trustee.

173.1

173.4

173.2

173.5

173.3

174.1

174.4

174.2

174.5

174.3

174.6

174.1
Kristin Breslin Sommese
Pennsylvania, 1993
Sommese Design
Anniversary logo for a regatta.

174.2
Bill Gardner/Sonia Greteman
Kansas, 1990
Gardner + Greteman
Anniversary logo for a community
arts celebration.

174.3
Eliza Tassian
Ohio, 1993
George Tassian Organization
Anniversary logo for Cincinnati's School
for the Creative and Performing Arts.

174.4
John Sayles
Iowa, 1993
Sayles Graphic Design
Anniversary logo for a leadership
conference.

174.5
Sharon Lejeune
Texas, 1992
David Carter Design
Logo for a restaurant.

174.6
Kevin Whaley
Minnesota, 1993
GrandPré and Whaley, Ltd.
AD: Lydia Anderson
Logo for an incentive program.

175.1
Kelly Allen
Texas, 1993
SullivanPerkins
AD: Ron Sullivan
Anniversary logo.

175.2
Lanny Sommese/
Kristin Breslin Sommese
Pennsylvania, 1988
Sommese Design
AD: Lanny Sommese
Anniversary logo.

175.3
Alan Colvin
Oregon, 1993
Nike Design
Illus: Alan Colvin/Lena James
Logo for a road race.

175.1

175.2

175.3

176.1

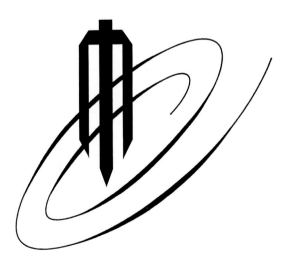

176.2

176.1
Michael Strassburger
Washington, 1992
Modern Dog
AD: Michael Strassburger/
Brent Turner/Luke Edgar
Logo for AC Snowboards.

176.2
Mary Cawein/Walter McCord
Kentucky, 1992
Choplogic
Personal logo for Mary Cawein.

177.1
John Heiden
California, 1989
John Heiden Design
Logo for Warner Bros. Records, to
represent the "cutting edge".

177.2
Margo Chase
California, 1993
Margo Chase Design
Logo for a CD cover.

177.3
Margo Chase
California, 1993
Margo Chase Design
Logo for Margo Chase Design.

177.4
Maureen Erbe
California, 1993
Maureen Erbe Design
Logo for a singer.

177.5
Jeanne Greco
New York, 1988
Parham Santana Inc.
AD: Maruchi Santana
Logo for a watch manufacturer.

Contemporary Music Department

177.1

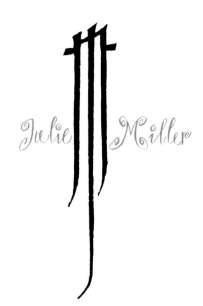

177.4

177.2

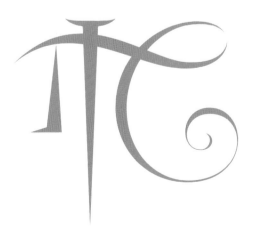

177.3

177.5

178.1

178.4

178.2

178.5

178.3

178.6

178.1
Rick Tharp/Kim Tomlinson
California, 1992
Tharp Did It
Logo for a restaurant,
the Blackhawk Grill

178.2
Steve Tolleson
California, 1992
Tolleson Design
Logo for Michael Tolleson Architecture.

178.3
Lorna Stovall
California, 1992
Lorna Stovall Design
AD: Elizabeth Barrett
Logo for Liz Laren CD cover.

178.4
Richard L. Baron
New Hampshire, 1992
Baron Graphics
Logo for a 60's style restaurant.

178.5
Renee Clark
Illinois, 1993
Renee Clark Design
Logo for an appliance repair business.

178.6
James A. Bearden
Iowa, 1993
Bearden Design
Logo for an organization of design
professionals, the IABC.

179.1
John Sayles
Iowa, 1993
Sayles Graphic Design
Personal logo,

179.2
Irene Yap
California, 1992
Evenson Design Group
AD: Stan Evenson
Proposed logo for California Literacy.

179.3
John Smeaton
California, 1993
The Mednick Group
AD: Scott Mednick/John Smeaton
Logo for a sports
memorabilia business.

179.1

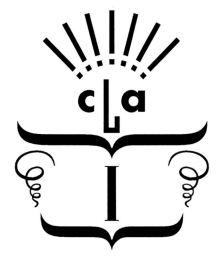

179.2

179.3

180.1

180.2

180.3

180.1
Bill Gardner/Sonia Greteman
Kansas, 1991
Gardner + Greteman
Logo for a civic organization
against gangs.

180.2
Daniel Riley
California, 1993
Riley Design Associates
An event logo for Hewlett Packard.

180.3
Greg Hoffman/Alan Colvin
Oregon, 1993
Nike Design
Event logo for an awards dinner.

181.1
Jeff Barnes
Illinois, 1985
Barnes Design
Logo for a high style gift store,

181.2
Tim Clark
New York, 1990
Tim Clark Design/Illustration
Logo for a furniture showroom,

181.3
Anonymous Graphics
Michigan, 1992
Logo for a recording company.

181.4
David Kampa
Texas, 1991
Kampa Design
AD: Betty Wong
Logo for a theatrical production.

181.1

181

FURNITURE

181.2

M°JAZ

181.3

181.4

182.1

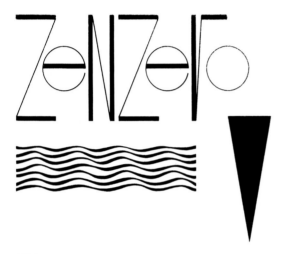

182.2

182.3

182.4

182.1
Pat Hansen
Washington, 1989
Hansen Design Company
Logo for a specialty chocolate company.

182.2
Francesca Garcia-Marques
California, 1992
Studio Francesca Garcia-Marques
Logo for a restaurant by the sea.

182.3
April Greiman
California, 1988
April Greiman Inc.
Logo for an interior design showroom.

182.4
Clive Piercy/Michael Hodgson
California, 1992
Ph.D
Logo for a fashion designer.

183.1
Don Sibley
Texas, 1993
Sibley/Peteet Design, Inc
Logo for an artists rep.

183.2
Jim Guerard
California, 1991
Robert Miles Runyan & Associates
Logo for a computerized retail sales
and inventory control system.

183.3
Jerry Balchunas
Rhode Island, 1993
Adkins Balchunas Design
Logo for an audio/video
production company.

183.4
Sean Adams/Noreen Morioka
California, 1991
Adams/Morioka
Logo for a Japanese clothing line.

183.5
John Clark
California, 1992
Looking
Logo for a graphic design studio.

183.6
Donald L. Kiel
New York, 1991
Swanke Hayden Connell Architects
Logo for a tire-recycling company.

JACQUELINE DeDELL Inc

183.1

OPTIMA

183.2

183.3

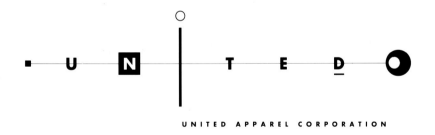

UNITED APPAREL CORPORATION

183.4

L O O K I N G

183.5

EPROTEK

183.6

184.1

184.2

184.3

184.4

184.5

184.1
Tom Antista/Petrula Vrontikis
California, 1989
Antista Design
Logo for fashion importers.

184.2
Pat Hansen
Washington, 1989
Hansen Design Company
Logo for a disco.

184.3
David Lemley
Washington, 1993
David Lemley Design
AD: Tawnya Crandall-Lemley
Logo for software.

184.4
Luis Fitch
Ohio, 1990
Luis Fitch Diseño
Logo for an electronics
equipment company.

184.5
Luis Fitch
Ohio, 1991
Luis Fitch Diseño
Logo for a satellite dish installer.

185.1-181.5
Walter McCord
Kentucky, 1988
Choplogic
Logos for a photography studio.

185.1

A

m

185.2

185.3

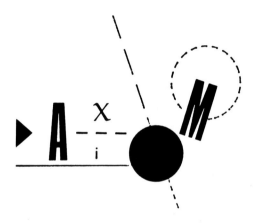

185.4

a

m

185.5

186.1

186.2

186.3

186.4

186.1
John Sayles
Iowa, 1993
Sayles Graphic Design
Event logo for an insurance company.

186.2
Kevin Whaley
Minnesota, 1992
GrandPré & Whaley, Ltd.
AD: Pat Wright
Logo for GTE/Power Moves, a
company incentive program.

186.3
Don Emery
Illinois, 1992
Mark Oldach Design
AD: Mark Oldach
Logo for the National Safety
Council's conference.

186.4
Luis Fitch
Ohio, 1989
Luis Fitch Diseño
Logo for a spicy drink.

187.1
Jennifer Morla, Sharrie Brooks
California, 1991
Morla Design
AD: Jennifer Morla
Logo for a video production facility.

187.2
Eric Atherton
California, 1992
Siegel & Gale Cross
AD: James Cross
Logo for a paper company's newsletter.

187.3
Mark Oldach
Illinois, 1991
Mark Oldach Design
Logo for Sourelis & Associates, business
consultants for graphic design firms.

187.4
Arnold Yew
Hawaii, 1993
Whodunit Design
Promotional logo for design firm.

187.5
April Greiman/Noreen Morioka
California, 1993
April Greiman, Inc.
Logo for a restaurant.

GOOD PICTURES

187.1

187.2

187.3

187.4

187.5

188.1

188.2

188.3

188.4

188.5

189.1

189.2

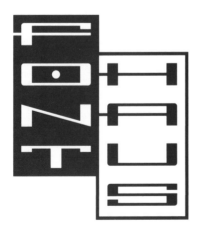

189.3

188.1
Jarin Taechanarong
California, 1992
Logo for Bangkok 1, a restaurant.

188.2
Margo Chase
California, 1993
Margo Chase Design
Logo for Toto CD cover.

188.3
James F. Kraus
Massachusetts, 1993
Art Guy Studios
Logo for a band.

188.4
Maureen Erbe
California, 1993
Maureen Erbe Design
Proposed logo for an office building.

188.5
Mark Sackett
California, 1991
Sackett Design
Illus: Chris Yaryan
Logo for an art gallery.

189.1
Wilson Ong
California, 1992
M Squared Design
AD: Marcus Hewitt
Promotional logo for a new sake.

189.2
Terry Lesniewicz
Ohio, 1990
Lesniewicz Associates, Inc.
Illus: Jack Bollinger
Logo for a contemporary jeweler.

189.3
Mark Fox
California, 1991
Black Dog
Logo for a postscript type retailer.

190.1

190.2

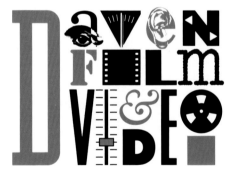

190.3

AGIT·PROP!

190.4

190.1
Dan Weeks
Ohio, 1992
Weeks & Associates
Logo for an up-scale techno dance club.

190.2
Mark Fox
California, 1992
Black Dog
AD: Tom O'Grady/NBA
Logo for the Detroit basketball team.

190.3
Earl Gee
California, 1991
Earl Gee Design
Logo for a film production firm.

190.4
Mark Fox
California, 1991
Black Dog
Logo for a typeface.

191.1
John Clark
California, 1993
Looking
Logo for a furniture manufacturer.

191.2
Katherine Lam
California, 1991
Patrick SooHoo Designers
Logo for the Acapulco Board of Tourism.

191.3
John Clark
California, 1990
Looking
Logo for a broad line of furniture.

191.4
Jeanne Greco
New York, 1992
Caffe Greco Design
AD: Sam Clayton
Logo for a line of iron furniture.

191.5
William Reuter/Michael Bain
California, 1993
William Reuter Design
Logo for a multimedia based
advertising agency

191.6
Leah Toby Hoffmitz
California, 1993
Letterform Design
Logo for security industry specialists.

191.7
Assis Mahdi
California, 1992
Upfront
Logo for a restaurant.

191.1

191.5

191.2

191.6

ARK

191.3

191.7

26

Fe ARC

191.4

192.1
John Heiden
California, 1990
John Heiden Design
AD: Jeff Fey
Logo for a CD cover.

192.2
Mike Quon
New York, 1991
Mike Quon Design Office
AD: Andre Tavernise
Logo for a hair salon.

192.3
John Heiden/Henk Elenga
California, 1987
John Heiden Design/
Hard Werken LA Desk
Promotional logo for the studios.

193.1
John Clark
California, 1993
Looking
Logo for fabricator of sets,
signs 'and displays.

193.2
Flavio Kampah
California, 1993
Kampah Visions
Logo for a broadcast design studio.

193.3
John Heiden
California, 1986
John Heiden Design
AD: Chuck Beeson
Logo for a record company.

193.4
Somi Kim/Whitney Lowe
California, 1992
ReVerb, Los Angeles
Logo for a magazine on the current arts.

192.1

192.2

192.3

193.1

193.2

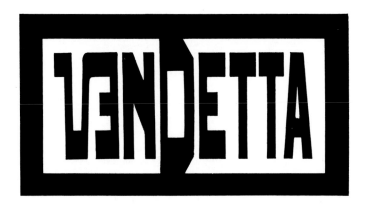

193.3

193.4

194.1

194.2

194.1
John Clark
California, 1992
Looking
Event logo celebrating the
anniversary of Futurism.

194.2
Craig Ferreirra
California, 1992
Logo for a catering company.

195.1
Patrice Eilts
Missouri, 1992
Eilts Anderson Tracy
Logo for a restaurant.

195.2
Joe Duffy
Minnesota, 1993
Duffy, Inc.
Logo for a financial services company.

195.3
MaeLin Levine
California, 1990
Visual Asylum
Logo for a photographic competition.

195.4
Jennifer Morla/Jeanette Aramburu
California, 1989
Morla Design
AD: Jennifer Morla
Logo for a clothing line.

195.5
Jeanne Greco/Stefan Sagmeister
New York, 1989
Parham Santana Inc.
AD: Maruchi Santana
Logo for a division of a watch company.

195.6
Kevin Flatt/John Swieter
Texas, 1992
Swieter Design
AD: John Swieter/Paul Munsterman
Illus: Kevin Flatt
Logo for a jazz band.

195.1

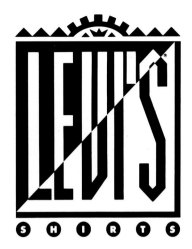

195.4

195.2

195.5

195.3

195.6

196.1

196.6

196.2

196.3

196.4

196.5

197.1

196.1-196.5
Marc DeBartolomeis
New York, 1991
Walker Group/CNI
Logos for department store departments.

196.6
Kristin Breslin Sommese
Pennslyvania, 1989
Sommese Design
Logo for a design studio.

197.1- 197.2
Gerald Reis/Albert Treskin
California, 1992
Gerald Reis & Company
Logo for columns in the Asian Art
Museum newsletter.

197.3
Emily Wong
California, 1991
M Design
Logo for a museum.

197.2

197.3

198.1

198.2

198.3

SPAZMSFASHION

198.4

198.1
Terrence Tong
California, 1992
Primo Angeli Inc.
AD: Ron Hoffman
Logo for a sports equipment company.

198.2
Scott Wampler
Illinois, 1992
Opal Arts
Logo for a jeweler who uses ethno-
graphic beads in his work.

198.3
Lanny Sommese
Pennsylvania, 1992
Sommese Design
Event logo for a picnic and softball game.

198.4
David Kampa
Texas, 1991
Kampa Design
AD: Larry Goode
Logo for a feature in Spazms magazine.

199.1
Margo Chase
California, 1993
Margo Chase Design
Logo for a design directory.

199.2
Lorna Stovall
California, 1993
Lorna Stovall Design
Logo for a men's sportswear line.

199.3
Jeff Weithman
Oregon, 1993
Nike Design
Illus: David Gill
Logo adapted for infants
footwear and apparel.

199.4
Walter McCord
Kentucky, 1986
Choplogic
Logo for a cafe and bakery.

199.5
Doug Zimmerman
Iowa, 1993
Younkers, Inc. Ad Department
Promotional logo for a clothing retailer.

199.6
Margo Chase
California, 1993
Margo Chase Design
Logo for a concert tour,
The Girlie Show, and inspired
by French carnival posters.

199.1

199.4

199.2

199.5

199.3

199.6

200.1

200.2

200.1
Margo Chase
California, 1992
Margo Chase Design
Logo for a hard rock, heavy metal band.

200.2
Wendy Behrens
Illinois, 1991
Wendy Behrens Design
Logo for a barber shop.

200.3
Jeanne Greco
New York, 1991
Caffé Greco Design
Logo for a screen writing firm.

200.4
Luis Fitch
Ohio, 1993
Luis Fitch Diseño
Logo for a record shop that special-
izes in Caribbean music.

200.3

200.4

DESIGNERS

201

DESIGN STUDIOS

ART DIRECTORS & ILLUSTRATORS

205

209

Introduction logos,
Page 9
top to bottom:

Robert Bruce Sweaters [1987]
Art Direction: Michael Toth
Design & Illustration: Michael Schwab
Agency: Toth Design, Inc.
Firm: Michael Schwab Design

Lone Star Donuts [1985]
Art Direction: Tom White, Rex Peteet
Design: Rex Peteet
Agency: Saunders, Lubinski & White
Firm: Sibley/Peteet Design, Inc.

The Good Diner [1992]
Design: Michael Bierut
Illustration: Woody Pirtle
Firm: Pentagram

Gotcha Sportswear [1985]
Design & Illustration: Jay Vigon
Firm: Vigon Seireeni

Time Warner [1990]
Art Direction: Steff Geissbuhler
Design: Steff Geissbuhler
Firm: Chermayeff & Geismar, Inc.

SPECIAL THANKS

I would like to thank my production assistant, Lisa Woodard for her outstanding perseverence against all odds in getting this book out. Also I would like to thank Joan Borgman and Anita Bennett for their help.

G.R.